DETAILING
FREIGHT CARS

Jeff Wilson

KALMBACH
BOOKS

About the author

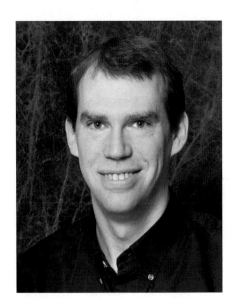

Detailing Freight Cars is Jeff Wilson's 18th book on railroads and model railroading. Jeff spent 10 years as an associate editor at *Model Railroader* magazine, and he currently works as a freelance writer, editor, and photographer, contributing articles to MR and other magazines. He also writes a model railroading column for *Model Retailer* magazine and is a correspondent for *Trains* magazine. He enjoys many facets of the hobby, especially building structures and detailing rolling stock and locomotives. He also enjoys photographing both real and model railroads.

Printed in the United States of America

11 10 09 08 07   1 2 3 4 5

Visit our Web site at kalmbachbooks.com.
Secure online ordering available.

Unless noted, photos were taken by the author.

Publisher's Cataloging-In-Publication Data
(Prepared by The Donohue Group, Inc.)

Wilson, Jeff, 1964-
    Detailing freight cars / Jeff Wilson.

    p. : ill. ; cm. -- (Model railroader's how-to guide)

    ISBN: 978-0-89024-691-7

1. Railroads--Freight-cars--Models. 2. Railroads--Freight-cars--Design and construction.
I. Title. II. Title: Freight cars

TF197 .W543 2007
625.194

Contents

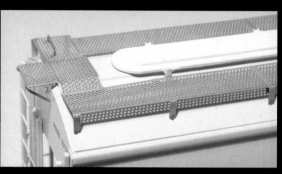

CHAPTER ONE

Freight car basics

Weathering and the addition of a few details to these HO plastic freight cars go a long way toward creating a realistic scene. The car at left has a resin detail kit from Sunshine Models; the other cars are by InterMountain.

Modelers tend to make locomotives the stars of their model railroads. However, improved quality of models, a growing variety of after-market detail items, and increased availability of prototype information have all helped spur interest in the accuracy of the entire train.

Kadee's ready-to-run PS-1 boxcar set a new standard for plastic freight car detailing when it was introduced in the mid-1990s.

Early days

In the early years of the hobby, the only affordable way to get a high-quality car was to build a craftsman-style metal or wood kit. Easy-to-build injection-molded styrene kits increased in quality and dropped in price in the 1950s and '60s. Injection-molding was an economical way to make cars by the thousands, but manufacturers didn't worry about capturing the many subtle differences found on cars from railroad to railroad, and even order by order.

In the 1970s, manufacturers including Detail Associates, Details West, and Tichy brought out a wide range of detail parts, allowing modelers to more easily customize their freight cars.

Other manufacturers began introducing limited-run, craftsman-style kits made from polyurethane resin. Specialized cars or railroad-specific versions of cars from Funaro & Camerlengo, Sunshine, Westerfield, and others featured separate detail items and resulted in well-detailed, realistic models, like the Burlington boxcar shown on page 4.

Kadee sparked a revolution in freight car modeling in the mid-1990s when it introduced its ready-to-run

model of a Pullman-Standard PS-1 boxcar, **1-1**. It was the first ready-to-run car that featured fine details such as see-through running boards; separate, thin-profile grab irons; sill

steps and ladders; and brake gear with underbody piping and rods; as well as end detail. Kadee also offered the car in several prototypical versions with different door styles and open-

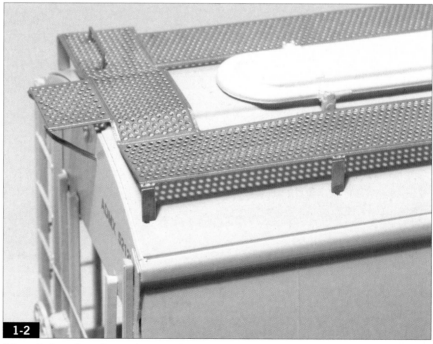

Athearn's Genesis-series model of a Trinity 5,161-cubic-foot covered hopper features etched-stainless-steel running boards and many separately applied details. It's typical of high-end, prototypical models available today.

ing widths and different brakewheels. Kadee brought out the car at the then-unheard-of price of $30, which many thought to be way too expensive for a plastic freight car.

However, Kadee was on the mark. The car sold well (and continues to do so), and showed the hobby world that modelers would pay a premium price for a highly detailed, realistic freight car. Since then, most other manufacturers, including Athearn Genesis, **1-2**, Atlas, Branchline, InterMountain, Proto 2000, and Red Caboose, have followed with their own high-end, ready-to-run cars.

Car quality

A trip to a local hobby shop will reveal a wide variety of models – and a variety of quality. Companies such as Bachmann, Life-Like, and Model Power still market inexpensive freight cars in train sets or as additions to sets, **1-3**.

Although their price might make them attractive, shortcomings include a lack of details such as brake gear; molded-on (instead of separate) ladders, grab irons, and running boards; and heavy or inaccurate details. They often have truck-mounted couplers, and their paint jobs are often unrealistic, with incorrect colors and lettering. The cars themselves often don't follow (or are a poor representation of) a specific prototype, with inaccurate dimensions and details.

Between these cars and the high-end offerings are a number of good kit and ready-to-run cars from Accurail, Athearn (Ready-to-Roll line), Bowser, C&BT Shops, and Walthers. These cars are generally accurate for their prototypes, but lack some of the high-end cars' detailing, such as brake rods and lines, or have some details molded in place. These cars generally have

accurate paint schemes and present great potential for upgrading.

What makes a freight car a good model? All of us have our own standards for "good enough." For some modelers, it means that every detail from the ladders to the running board style, and on to the paint scheme, must match its prototype. Others are happy as long as the paint scheme looks good.

For most of us, concern about fidelity to the real thing increases the longer we stay in the hobby. As our knowledge of the prototype grows and our modeling skills improve, our perception of what makes a good model tends to rise.

Resources

Even with the high quality of models now available, there are many ways of improving cars with additional details, decals, and weathering. You don't have to go overboard: Enhance new cars as

1-3

Train set-quality cars, such as this Life-Like hopper, typically have oversize molded-on details and truck-mounted couplers and lack separate detail parts. The paint and lettering also usually aren't up to the quality of high-end models.

1-4

Valuable references include (clockwise from top left) a *Car Builders' Cyclopedia*, an issue of the *Official Railway Equipment Register*, one of Morning Sun's color equipment guides, and a Burlington Route Historical Society publication on 40-foot boxcars.

you acquire them and upgrade your existing fleet as you can.

The parts used throughout this book are listed with numbers, but it's impossible to provide a complete list of all detail parts and decals available, much less information on all of the hundreds of freight car models and variations produced. To see what's out there, visit a well-stocked hobby shop. Also, look through the Walthers catalogs and Web site and check out the catalogs and Web sites of individual manufacturers as well.

For more information on prototype freight cars, look at books like *The Model Railroader's Guide to Freight Cars* (published by Kalmbach). The numerous railroad-specific and car-type-specific color books from Morning Sun and others are great references for determining what details are correct for specific freight cars, **1-4**, especially for the late steam and early diesel eras.

The *Official Railway Equipment Register* is a quarterly publication that lists every freight car in service in North America. The *ORER* is a great reference for checking car numbers and dimensional data and determining when cars were in service. It also includes notes on American Association of Railroads' car designations and plate clearances.

The *Car Builders' Cyclopedia*, published every few years, provides drawings and information on freight cars. Many larger libraries have them, and you can also look for them (and *ORER*s) on eBay and through paper dealers specializing in railroadiana.

Many railroad historical societies publish magazines and books on their railroad's freight cars. *Freight Cars Journal* is a periodical devoted to the cars themselves.

Hobby magazines such as *Model Railroader*, *Mainline Modeler*, *Model Railroading*, *RailModel Journal*, and *Railroad Model Craftsman* include articles on freight car modeling, often with drawings and reference material. The magazine index on the trains.com Web site is a handy reference for tracking down articles from these and other magazines.

CHAPTER TWO

Wheels, trucks, and couplers

Good wheels and trucks are important for looks and operation. This HO scale Kato model of a solid-bearing ASF A-3 Ride Control truck has been weathered following guidelines in Chapter 7.

Choosing the right couplers, trucks, and wheels makes a big difference in the operation and appearance of freight cars, making it a good idea to start upgrading cars from the ground up. These components are also among the easiest freight car improvements, with a number of after-market components available.

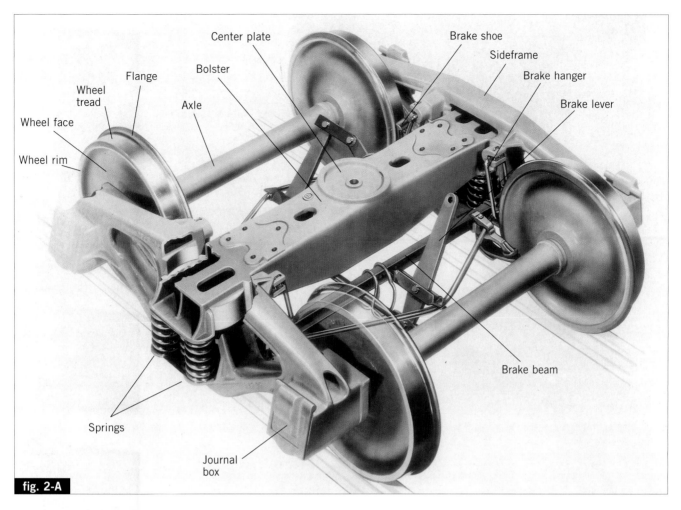

Center plate

Brake shoe

Sideframe

Bolster

Brake hanger

Flange

Brake lever

Wheel tread

Axle

Wheel face

Wheel rim

Brake beam

Springs

Journal box

fig. 2-A

Trucks and wheels

Most freight cars ride on four-wheel trucks, which are complex assemblies with many components, as **Figure 2-A** shows. Model trucks are much simpler. Most use single-piece plastic castings that include the sideframes and bolster, holding a pair of needlepoint wheelsets. In HO scale, Kadee makes multi-piece metal trucks with separate

springs, and some manufacturers offer trucks cast in brass.

Some model cars have plastic wheelsets, some with the wheels and axle cast as a single piece, and others with plastic wheels pressed on metal axles. Higher-quality wheelsets feature metal wheels pressed onto plastic needlepoint axles.

Prototype trucks are either solid-bearing or roller-bearing. Solid-bearing

trucks (often incorrectly called friction-bearing), **2-1**, were standard into the 1960s. Journal boxes over the wheel bearings hold oil-impregnated cotton waste, **2-2**, which keeps the bearing surfaces lubricated. Although cheaper than roller bearings, these trucks were maintenance intensive, requiring frequent lubrication, and if a bearing went dry, a hotbox followed by a fire or axle

2-1

The Barber S-2 was one of the most common trucks from World War II into the 1960s.

2-2

The journal box holds cotton waste impregnated with oil, which keeps the bearing surfaces lubricated. Note the oil residue on the wheel face.

2-3

Roller-bearing trucks are now standard; 100-ton trucks like this one have three springs visible. The end caps on the roller bearings rotate with the wheels.

failure was the result if the problem wasn't noticed quickly.

Roller-bearing trucks, **2-3**, solved this by using sealed roller bearings over the axle ends. These trucks have distinctive roller-bearing end caps in place of journal boxes. Passenger cars began using roller bearings in large numbers in the 1930s, but they didn't gain wide use on freight cars until the 1960s.

Roller bearing trucks became mandatory on new equipment in 1968, and many older cars received them from the 1960s through the 1990s. Roller bearings were required on all cars in interchange service in 1995.

Wheels have also evolved. Through the steam era, many prototype wheels were made of cast iron. Called "chilled" wheels because of the heat treatment

they received, their backs were often ribbed to aid in cooling during braking. Cast and wrought steel wheels had fewer problems, and iron wheels were prohibited on new cars after 1957 and banned from interchange in 1970.

Cars with capacities up to 70 tons ride on 33"-diameter wheels, except for low-profile flatcars used for triple-deck auto racks, which use distinctive 28"-diameter wheels. Modern 100- and 110-ton cars ride on 36" wheels, and some intermodal cars with 125-ton capacity use 38" wheels.

Truck styles and models

Trucks in the two basic categories – solid bearing and roller bearing – came in many different styles. Fortunately for modelers, manufacturers offer many of these variations in miniature. The chart on page 21 lists many of the trucks available in HO and N scales.

Archbar trucks were the most common type into the early 1900s, **2-4**. These used pressed steel components, bolted together. They were superceded by trucks with cast sideframes, starting with the Bettendorf T-section truck,

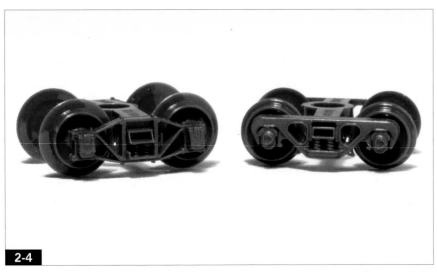

2-4

Micro-Trains N scale trucks include archbar (no. 1011) and 70-ton roller-bearing (no. 1006). Both are molded in engineering plastic.

2-5

Kadee HO trucks, including this Bettendorf T-section (no. 512), feature metal sideframes, real springs, and metal wheels.

2-6

Accurail's HO Andrews trucks have plastic sideframes and plastic (no. 103) or metal (no. 203) wheels.

2-5, through the 1910s. Andrews trucks, **2-6**, became popular from this period through the 1930s. They had cast sideframes, but used bolted-on journal boxes, many re-used from old archbar trucks.

Single-piece cast sideframes continued to evolve in the '20s, with a U-shaped cross section for increased strength. This design was adopted as a standard by the ARA (American Railway Association) and later AAR

(American Association of Railroads), **2-7**. ARA and AAR trucks were the most common through the steam era. Although incorrectly referred to generically as "Bettendorf" trucks, several manufacturers built them. Other popular early trucks included the Dalman and Gould designs.

The two most common designs from World War II into the 1960s were the Barber S-2, **2-1**, and the most popular, the ASF A-3 Ride Control

(see page 8). These trucks improved ride quality and eliminated the spring plank (the long platform that extended from sideframe to sideframe under the springs). Other trucks advertising improved riding characteristics were the National B-1, with its unique spring/bolster design, **2-8**, and the Allied Full Cushion, which was popular on express boxcars from the 1940s into the mid-1950s, when that style was banned from interchange.

2-7

The AAR cast truck (this one built by Bettendorf) has a sideframe with a U-shaped cross section. This style of truck with a spring plank under the springs and connecting the two sideframes was a popular choice on freight cars into the 1940s.

2-8

The appearance of the distinctive National B-2 is captured well by this Proto 2000 HO model (no. 920-21254).

2-9

This HO scale Proto 2000 model (no. 920-21256) represents a 100-ton Barber S-2 roller-bearing truck, one of the most commonly used today.

2-10

The two visible springs mark this as a 70-ton version of the ASF Ride Control truck. The Athearn HO model (no. G4598) has end caps that actually rotate.

The most common trucks in use today are 70- and 100-ton roller-bearing versions of the Barber S-2, 2-9, and ASF A-3, 2-10. In general, 70-ton trucks have two visible springs, and 100-ton trucks have three. The style of end caps also varies among trucks.

Athearn and Kato offer HO scale roller-bearing truck models with rotating end caps, 2-10. Both use special needle-end axles, with the caps fitting on the tips of axles. These make for distinctive models, capturing the motion of real trucks.

Model wheelsets

Several companies, including Atlas (HO and N), InterMountain (HO and N), Jay-Bee (HO), Kadee (HO), Kato (HO), Micro-Trains (N), NorthWest Short Line (HO), Proto 2000 (HO), and ReBoxx (HO), offer replacement wheelsets. Most use metal wheels, which tend to stay cleaner and help to clean and polish the railheads as they move. Metal wheels also add to a car's weight (about a half ounce for four wheelsets in HO), which lowers the car's center of gravity. Metal wheels also look much better than plastic.

In HO scale, semi-scale wheelsets (with an .088"-wide tread) have become popular, 2-11. These have a more-realistic look than the wide-tread (.110") wheels and will still operate well on most track. Scale-width wheelsets, 2-11, are available from NorthWest Short Line and others. These look great, but will drop into gaps on turnouts on most commercial track. If in doubt, test your

2-11

Replacement HO needlepoint-axle metal wheelsets from top to bottom: Kadee 33" (no. 520), InterMountain 33" semi-scale (no. 40052), and NorthWest Short Line 33" scale-width (no. 57617-4).

track with a truck fitted with wheelsets you'd like to use.

Wheels are available in all diameters used on the prototype, and many manufacturers make wheels with ribbed backs to represent prototype iron wheels.

Micro-Trains N scale wheelsets are plastic, but Atlas and InterMountain offer metal replacements. Micro-Trains sells (and includes with its cars) wheels with both deep and shallow flanges, **2-4**. The shallow ones look much better and will run just fine.

Replacing trucks and wheels

To replace a car's trucks, unscrew the original and substitute the new one in its place. Tighten truck screws until

you can't turn the trucks easily, then back off a half turn. If a car wobbles, tighten just one of the screws until the wobble disappears.

New wheelsets can be added to trucks by pulling the sideframes apart slightly, slipping out the old wheelsets, and popping in the new ones, **2-12**.

If the wheelsets bind and don't roll smoothly, you can often fix them by reaming out the axle-end pockets on plastic sideframes, **2-13**. Micro-Mark offers a tool, the Truck Tuner (no. 82838), to do this for HO models. It will remove any stray flash and shape the cone properly. (Don't do this with drill bits – they will cut into the plastic.) You can also try wheelsets with different-length axles. ReBoxx

and NorthWest Short Line offer HO wheelsets in varying axle lengths.

Smooth operations rely on wheelsets that are gauged properly. Use a National Model Railroad Association standards gauge (available from many hobby shops or directly from the NMRA) for your scale to check wheelsets for gauge, **2-14**. If you find a wheelset out of gauge, it can usually be corrected by grabbing each wheel and twisting it into gauge, **2-15**.

Couplers

Horn-hook couplers came as standard equipment on most HO scale ready-to-run and kit freight cars into the 1990s (photo **1-3**) as did the Rapido coupler in N scale, **2-16**. These couplers were

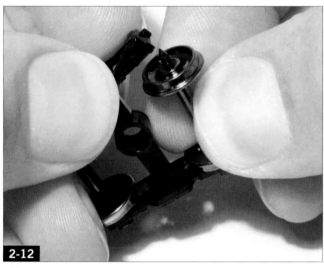

2-12

To remove or replace a wheelset, pull the sideframe apart slightly and slip the wheelset in place.

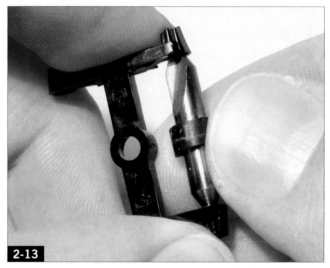

2-13

Micro-Mark's Truck Tuner reams out the needlepoint pockets on HO truck sideframes, removing flash and improving operation.

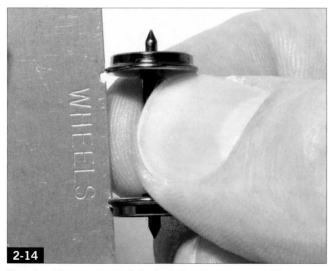

2-14

The wheel flanges should fit in the "wheel" slots on an NMRA standards gauge. This wheelset is wide in gauge.

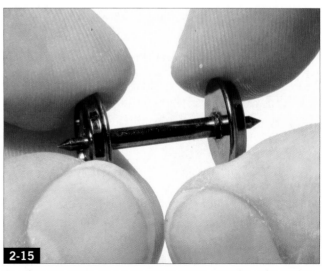

2-15

To adjust the gauge, grab both wheels firmly and twist while pulling or pushing them on the axle.

2-16

The N scale Rapido coupler works by the wedge-shaped front edges riding over each other.

inexpensive to produce, and any company could make them.

Although cheap and plentiful, both suffer operationally and visually: Neither looks anything like a real coupler. Although both work reasonably well for coupling, they can be difficult to uncouple, and truck-mounted horn-hooks tend to skew cars to the side when pushed.

Enter the Kadee Magne-Matic coupler, **2-17**. Available in N (now by Micro-Trains), HO, S, O, and large

scale versions, these couplers resemble real couplers and operate smoothly. Uncoupling can be accomplished manually by inserting a pick between the knuckles and twisting, or automatically by using a magnetic uncoupling ramp placed between the rails or under the track. The magnet forces the steel uncoupling pins (the curved pieces hanging below the coupler) apart, opening the knuckles and allowing the cars to be pulled apart without touching them.

In the 1990s, as many of Kadee's patents expired, other companies began making automatic knuckle couplers that mate with Magne-Matics. Today, Accurail (Accumate), McHenry, **2-18**, Bachmann (E-Z Mate), and Proto 2000 all offer automatic knuckle couplers.

The latest trend is toward scale-size couplers in HO scale, with Kadee's no. 58 (**2-17**), Accurail's scale Accumate, and McHenry's scale coupler. All provide improved appearance, although

2-17

Kadee's all-metal no. 5 coupler, left, has been the hobby's de facto standard for decades, and the scale-size no. 58 coupler, right, has grown rapidly in popularity since its release a few years ago.

2-18

McHenry's KS-series couplers have a plastic shank and knuckle, steel uncoupling pin, and metal coil knuckle spring.

the shallower mating faces mean installation must be precise.

Most freight car models today come with some type of knuckle coupler, meaning less need for adding replacements. However, you'll still find it handy to retrofit couplers on some cars. Some modelers prefer scale couplers on all equipment; others prefer using a single brand of coupler.

Coupler selection is largely a matter of personal preference. Kadee remains a popular choice, as its metal couplers have a well-earned reputation for reliability and dependable operation. Also, Kadee offers dozens of coupler styles with varying mounting styles, including different shaft lengths as well as overset and underset couplers, **2-19**.

McHenry, Proto 2000, and E-Z Mate HO couplers work in much the same way as Magne-Matic couplers. Accumate couplers have a split-shank design that relies on springs in the coupler box to close the knuckle. All have plastic shanks.

Some early versions of these couplers used plastic leaf knuckle springs, and some are still available. These couplers proved troublesome; if a knuckle is held in the open position (such as in a storage box or bunched with other cars on a track), the spring will take a set in that position and no longer close

the knuckle. Although metal knuckle-spring couplers might cost a bit more, I strongly recommend them.

In N scale, Micro-Trains Magne-Matic couplers remain the de facto standard. They, along with Accumate's N scale version, use a split-shank design. They're available mounted on the firm's trucks, as well as in several kit and assembled versions for mounting directly on cars.

Adjusting couplers

Regardless of the brand used, couplers must be installed properly to operate reliably.

All couplers must be mounted at the same height to operate well, especially with couplers in the smaller scales. Get a Kadee coupler-height gauge, **2-20**, and use it to check all couplers before placing cars in service.

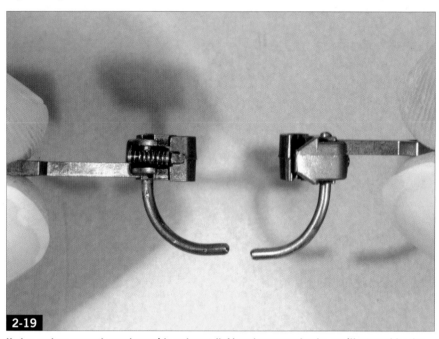

2-19

Kadee makes several couplers with underset (left) and overset shanks, as illustrated by the nos. 21 and 22 couplers.

2-20

The Kadee height gauge is invaluable for checking coupler installation. This Proto 2000 flatcar has a low coupler.

Place the coupler gauge on the track (with no power on, since the gauge is metal and will cause a short-circuit). Roll a car toward the gauge. The top of the car's coupler should be at the same height as the coupler on the gauge. If it's not, **2-20**, it must be adjusted to match.

You can make minor adjustments to a low coupler by adding washers between the truck and car bolster, **2-21**. Kadee makes fiber washers in .005" and .010" thicknesses to do this in HO.

Be aware that using more than two of these risks raising the car to an unprototypical height.

Another solution is to use a coupler with an underset or overset shank, **2-19** and **2-22**. Kadee and other companies

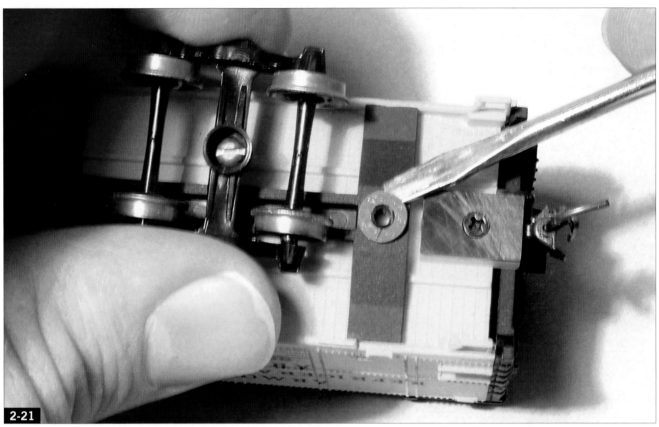

2-21

Kadee fiber washers can be added to car bolsters to raise coupler height.

2-22

A Kadee no. 27 coupler with an underset shank corrected the height problem on this Proto 2000 car.

make several couplers with shanks mounted higher and lower than standard couplers. Keep a few of these on hand for special applications.

Before adjusting a coupler, determine if the coupler itself is low (most likely), **2-20**, or if the coupler is sagging, **2-23**. If a coupler is sagging, the most likely cause is that the coupler shank isn't as thick as the space allowed in the coupler box. You can replace the coupler with a different brand, but if the box itself is simply too big, you can fix it by adding a thin (.005" or .010") styrene shim to the inside of the coupler box cover, **2-24** and **2-25**.

The uncoupling pin should clear the flat steel plate at the bottom of the

2-23

The coupler in this HO Athearn double-stack car isn't low – it's sagging.

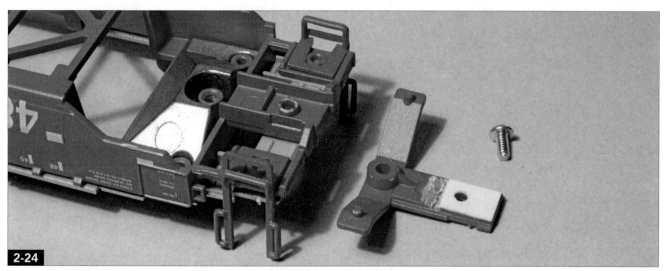

2-24

A thin styrene shim on the coupler-box cover, drilled for the mounting hole, tightens the space.

2-25

The coupler is now level – and the uncoupling pin has been fixed as well.

gauge. If it doesn't, it will likely catch on grade crossings and turnout closure rails. Kadee and Micro-Mark make pliers with special tips for bending trip pins to proper shape, **2-26**.

Installing couplers

Replacing couplers has become much simpler in recent years, as coupler boxes on most freight cars are sized to fit Kadee no. 5 and no. 58 and comparable couplers, **2-27**. In many cases, adding a new coupler is as simple as removing the box cover and swapping the couplers.

On many cars, friction pins hold the coupler box covers in place. These

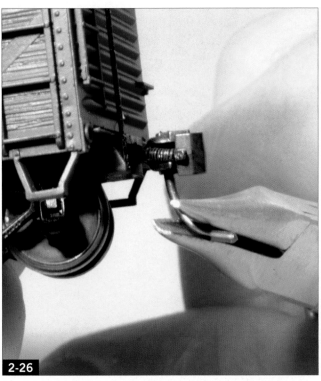

2-26

Special pliers make it easy to bend uncoupling pins up or down.

2-27

Coupler boxes on most HO cars, like this Proto 2000 flatcar, are sized for Kadee no. 5 couplers and bronze centering springs.

2-28

Drill out the box mounting hole, as on this Accurail boxcar, then tap it for a 2-56 mounting screw.

2-29

The screw holds the cover securely in place. Black paint helps hide the screwhead from view.

can fall out during operation, so many modelers replace the pins with screws. Screws hold the cover securely in place and can be removed easily to fix or replace a coupler.

To do this, cut off the friction pin from the cover and mark the center of the location with a pin or awl. Drill a clearance hole for the screw in the cover. I like to use 1-72 or 2-56 screws for HO (see the drill/clearance chart). Drill the coupler box with the proper-size hole for the screw.

Then tap the hole in the car for the screw by slowly turning the tap into the hole and backing it out to clear debris, **2-28**. The tap cuts the threads, making it easy to turn the screw into place. Install the coupler and screw the cover into place. A bit of black paint on the screw head helps to hide it, **2-29**.

You can also mount couplers in their own coupler boxes. To do this, make sure the underside of the car is level. You might have to remove the existing coupler box and any other moldwork from the center of the underside, **2-30**.

Test-fit the new coupler box, then drill an appropriate mounting hole, **2-31**. I used a Details West coupler box to hold a Kadee coupler to provide a more-realistic mounting for the HO Con-Cor refrigerator car in the sidebar on cushion draft gear on page 20.

It may take some experimenting to discover which couplers work best

Drill and tap

This reference will help you drill the proper size hole for the tap and clearance holes.

You can easily keep track of the appropriate drill bits for coupler installation (and other uses) by using a double-ended pin vise. Simply keep the tap in one end and the appropriate bit in the other, and you'll never dig through your workbench to find the right one again. I keep these for both 2-56 and 1-72 taps, the ones I most often use.

Screw size	Tap drill no.	Clearance drill no.
0-80	56	51
1-72	53	47
2-56	50	42
3-48	47	36

This double-ended pin vise from Mascot keeps a matching tap and drill together.

2-30

Use a hobby knife or Micro-Mark detail chisel to remove the old coupler box from the underside of the floor. Make sure the area is level.

2-31

The new coupler box must be centered properly. This Details West box has a cover that will screw in place onto the box.

on what cars. Micro-Trains offers the *Coupler Conversion Guide* in N scale, a handy reference for choosing and installing its couplers, and Kadee offers similar guides on its Web site.

Kadee's HO coupler sample kits are very handy for experimenting with various types of installations. The no. 13 kit includes one each of 25 different Kadee couplers.

When properly installed, the coupler shank should move freely from side to side and freely return to center. If a coupler sticks, check to make sure that the box is free of debris, that all inner surfaces are smooth and free of flash, and that the mounting screw isn't too tight. Never use oil or grease in a coupler box. Instead, you can use a small amount of powdered graphite such as Kadee Greas'em.

Replacing knuckle springs

The most common repair required on knuckle couplers seems to be replacing the knuckle spring. These tiny springs are fragile, and occasionally they catch on something and pop out of place, usually never to be seen again. The easiest way I've found to replace them is using a no. 11 knife blade. Press the blade gently into a coil at one end of the spring to hold it. Use the blade to place the spring over one mounting peg, then slip it over the other one and gently pull the knife away.

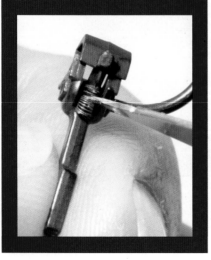

Cushion draft gear

Many prototype cars are equipped with underframe or end-of-car cushioning devices to protect freight loads. These use hydraulics or springs to absorb shock from slack action and hard coupling. You'll find them on some boxcars, refrigerator cars, and flatcars. Draft gear extends from the car ends at different lengths depending upon their spring travel, giving cars a distinctive look.

In HO scale, Details West makes several cushion pockets to match various prototypes. I used the no. 1023 pocket on a 57-foot Con-Cor Pacific Fruit Express reefer. Start by removing the model's coupler box and shave the area smooth with a hobby knife and chisel. Make sure the top of the box is centered, then drill a mounting hole and tap it for the mounting screw. The mounting hole for the bottom of the box must also be drilled and tapped into the top half of the box. Test-fit it before adding the coupler.

The finished installation is shown below. Details West also offers nicely detailed standard coupler boxes that closely resemble those of prototype cars.

It's easy to spot a car with cushioned draft gear, as the draft-gear box extends from the end of the car.

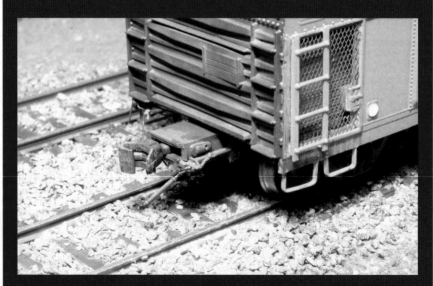

The Details West coupler box, combined with a Cal-Scale brake hose, captures the look of real cushioned draft gear.

HO scale — Solid-bearing trucks

Manufacturer	Archbar	Andrews	Vulcan double-truss	Bettendorf T-section	ARA, AAR	50-ton spring plankless	ASF A-3 Ride Control	Dalman	National B-1	Allied Full Cushion	Barber S-2
Accurail		103, 203			100, 200						
Athearn					90400						
Atlas					185000						
Bethlehem	134, 135, 1209, 1215	1227	1220	1204	1202			1224	1225		
Con-Cor					99250 99251						
Eastern Car Works**		9066 9067	9068		9053			9061	9057	9043	
InterMountain							40061				
Kadee†	501 503*	509 510*	515 516*	511 512*	500 502*			504			
Kato							31601				
Old Pullman†		40011 40061			40001 40081						
On-Trak	5304										
Proto 2000		920-23207				920-21251 920-21253			920-21254 920-21255		
Red Caboose		5007		5004							5016
Tichy	3002	3012			3024						
Walthers	933-1002 933-1010 933-1018	933-1004		933-1003 933-1011 933-1009	933-1001 933-1012 933-1008						

HO scale — Roller-bearing trucks

Manufacturer	70-ton roller-bearing	100-ton roller-bearing	70-ton Barber S-2	100-ton Barber S-2	70-ton ASF Ride Control	100-ton ASF Ride Control
Accurail				102, 202		
Athearn		90401			4598	4599
Atlas	180000	195000				
Con-Cor			99200 99220	99221		
Eastern Car Works**	9064		9054	9070		
InterMountain				40001 40060		
Kadee†		513	518			
Kato			31602			
Old Pullman†	40021 40091	40031				
Proto 2000				920-21256		
Walthers	933-1005	933-1013				

This is a summary of the most popular and common truck types available. It is not a comprehensive list of all trucks available. Check the Web sites and product catalogs of the various companies for details, including wheel type (metal or plastic), and for additional models.

* Truck-mounted coupler

† Kadee and Old Pullman trucks are sprung.

** Eastern Car Works truck kits do not contain wheelsets.

N scale

Manufacturer	Solid-bearing						Roller-bearing	
	Archbar	Andrews	ARA, AAR	National B-1	Allied Full Cushion	Dalman	70-ton	100-ton
Atlas			22050 22051*				22055 22056*	22070 22071*
InterMountain			60001*					60011*
Kato								800091
Micro-Trains	302001* 302004* 1012*	302015 302012* 302016*	302021* 302022* 302020	302151*	302121*	302162*	302031* 302034* 302030	302041* 302044* 302040
Model Die Casting	8984*		8983*				8980*	

Side sill

Crossbearer

Pipe to retaining valve

Center sill

Stringer

Train line

Rod to brake wheel

Control valve

Brake rods

Cylinder

Piston

Reservoir

Lever

CHAPTER THREE

Brake gear

This boxcar has a fairly typical layout of AB brake components.

Modeling the underside of a freight car might seem like a waste of time. However, much of a car's brake system, including brake lines, rods, and other hardware, is clearly visible from low-level views. Adding these details will help increase the realism of almost any model.

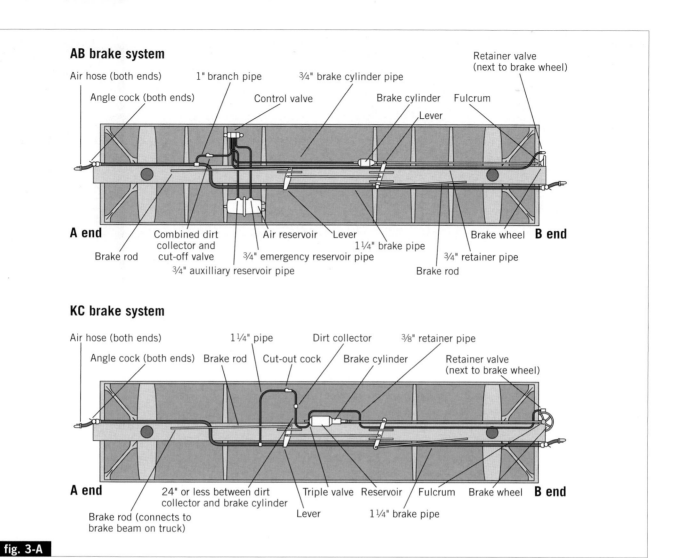

AB brake system

Air hose (both ends) — 1" branch pipe — ¾" brake cylinder pipe — Retainer valve (next to brake wheel)

Angle cock (both ends) — Control valve — Brake cylinder — Fulcrum — Lever

A end

Combined dirt collector and cut-off valve — Air reservoir — Lever — Brake wheel — B end

Brake rod — ¾" emergency reservoir pipe — 1¼" brake pipe — ¾" retainer pipe

¾" auxilliary reservoir pipe — Brake rod

KC brake system

Air hose (both ends) — 1¼" pipe — Dirt collector — ⅜" retainer pipe

Angle cock (both ends) — Brake rod — Cut-out cock — Brake cylinder — Retainer valve (next to brake wheel)

A end

24" or less between dirt collector and brake cylinder — Triple valve — Reservoir — Fulcrum — Brake wheel — B end

Brake rod (connects to brake beam on truck) — Lever — 1¼" brake pipe

fig. 3-A

Prototype brakes

Understanding how real brakes work makes it easier to figure out how to model brake details. **Figure 3-A** shows typical layouts of brake gear for 40- or 50-foot boxcars of the 1940s. Other cars use the same equipment, but the layout varies depending on the space available.

The AB brake system, shown on the opposite page, became the standard in 1933, and its successors (ABD in 1963, ABDW in 1976) look similar and work much the same way but with faster response time. Here's how the AB system works: The train line (or brake pipe) is the main air supply for the train. Each car is connected by hoses to adjoining cars, and each car has a branch from the train line to its control valve (not triple valve). The train line is charged with air during operation – usually at 70 to 90

pounds – and each car's control valve allows its reservoir to be filled with air from the line.

To apply the brakes, the engineer reduces the pressure in the train line. As each control valve senses this drop in pressure, it routes a proportionate amount of air from the reservoir to the brake cylinder, extending the piston from the cylinder. The end of the piston is connected to a lever, which via rods and another lever connects to the brake beams on each truck. As the piston extends, the brake shoes press against the wheel treads.

A car's brakes can also be set by its brake wheel. A rod runs from the end of the cylinder piston to the end of the car, where a fulcrum connects to a vertical rod that extends to the brake wheel. Turning the brake wheel pulls out the piston and applies the brakes.

Brake gear wire sizes, HO scale

Part	Size	Wire size
Train line (brake pipe)	1¼"	.019" (2506)
Retainer line	⅜"	.008" (2502)
Other pipes	¾"	.012" (2504)
Brake rods	⅞"	.010" (2503)

Pipe sizes are inside diameter; wire size reflects outside diameter. Detail Associates part number is in parentheses.

Triple valve

YOUNG VALVE

Dirt collector

Reservoir

REPACKED BY C&M.T.C. 8 25 31

Cylinder

INDIAN REFINING COMPANY. LESSEE

Lever

3-1

KC brakes, as on this tank car, had a combined cylinder, reservoir, and triple valve.

Another pipe runs from the control valve to the end of the car (next to the brake wheel), ending at the retainer valve. When activated – called "setting retainers" – some air is kept in the brake cylinder even when brakes are released, a handy feature in mountainous terrain.

A modern adaptation is the truck-mounted brake cylinder. These began appearing in 1970, and now many open-frame cars (tank cars, double-stack cars, covered hoppers) use them, avoiding under-car brake rods.

The K brake system was the standard into the 1930s, and many cars kept their K brakes through the 1940s. All interchange cars except tank cars were required to have AB brakes by 1949, with tank cars following by 1953.

Figure 3-A shows the KC (K combined) system, the most common K variation, which had the cylinder, reservoir, and triple valve together, **3-1**. The other version was the KD, with separate components. The K brake system functioned much the same way as the

AB, but with slower reaction time and no separate emergency air supply in the reservoir.

Modeling

Almost all kit and ready-to-run models today include the cylinder, control valve, and reservoir, and many come complete with underbody and end brake gear including rods and piping.

Brake sets are available from several makers in HO, **3-2**, including Cal-Scale (AB no. 283, KC no. 291, ABD

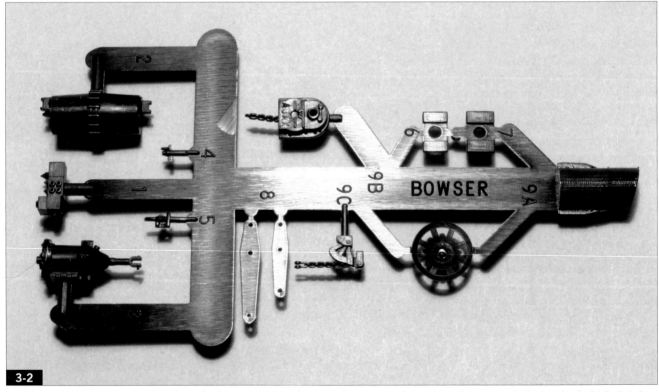

3-2

Cal-Scale's HO AB brake set includes the major components as well as rods, levers, a retainer valve, a fulcrum, and a brake wheel with its housing.

no. 313), Detail Associates (AB no. 6227, ABDXL no. 6247), and Tichy (AB no. 3013, KC no. 3005, split K no. 3034), and Precision Scale offers an AB set in N scale (no. 6712).

For a contest-quality model, you might add every piece of pipe and rod that can be seen on a real car. However, if you're just trying to capture the effect of brake gear, you can model just the parts that are visible from the sides.

Brakes on a boxcar

Adding underbody brake lines and piping is a relatively simple upgrade. You can keep a car's components, as I did on the Accurail HO car in the photos, or substitute with a commercial set. The chart on page 23 lists appropriate wire sizes to match the various prototype rods and pipes in HO scale.

The first step is to drill out the parts to accept the wire, **3-3**. Use a pin vise with a bit slightly larger than the wire size. Some components, such as

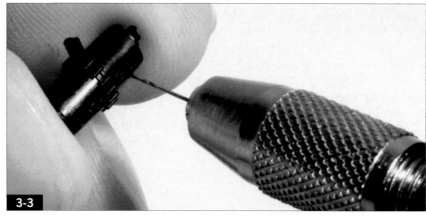

3-3 Drill out the components with a pin vise. The bit should be slightly larger than the wire size.

Cal-Scale's, have dimple locators at drill marks; for others, you'll have to estimate appropriate spots. Drill a hole at the non-piston end of the cylinder, two holes in the reservoir, and three to five holes in the control valve (depending upon how much of the piping you choose to add).

Glue on the valve and place the reservoir, but don't glue it yet. Begin

cutting wire to fit – in this case, the .012" wire between the reservoir and valve, **3-4**. Once the wires fit, dip each end into a drop of cyanoacrylate adhesive (CA) before placing them into the appropriate holes.

With the pipes between the valve, cylinder, and reservoir in place, glue on the cylinder and reservoir, **3-5**. I omitted the train line, the line to the retaining

3-4 Begin fitting the wire between each of the components. Use a fine needlenose pliers to insert the wire into the holes.

3-5 Glue small pieces of .010" styrene to the center sill, then glue the levers to them.

valve, and the rod to the brake wheel because they would be hidden from view.

Next comes the rodding. Start with the lever that connects to the end of the cylinder's piston, **3-5**. I used Cal-Scale levers, but you can cut your own from .010" sheet styrene.

Add the second lever, the rod connecting the levers, and the rods that extend from the levers to the trucks. Since connecting them to brake beams on model trucks isn't practical, glue these rods in place on the center sill next to the bolster, **3-6**.

Add the brackets over the levers, **3-6**. You can use commercial 18" grab irons, or bend your own from .010" or .012" brass wire. The underframe is now ready to paint and add to the car. You can see a photo of the finished car on page 30.

Center-beam brakes

Modern cars can be treated in the same manner. The Walthers HO center-beam flatcar (see chapter 8), based on a Thrall prototype, is a realistic model, but lacks brake rods and piping apparent on the prototype cars (see page 82).

Adding underbody gear was a bit more of a challenge because the car's floor, center sill, and cross members are die-cast metal. Instead of drilling holes, I used brackets that straddle the center sill and glued them in place with CA, **3-7**. The distinctive vertical brake lever (from the Cal-Scale set) fits into a notch in the sill.

The rod from this lever goes under the axles and is mounted in a hole drilled on the coupler-box cover. Be sure this wire doesn't interfere with the truck motion.

3-6

Add the rods, gluing the ends to the center sill at the bolster, then add the brackets.

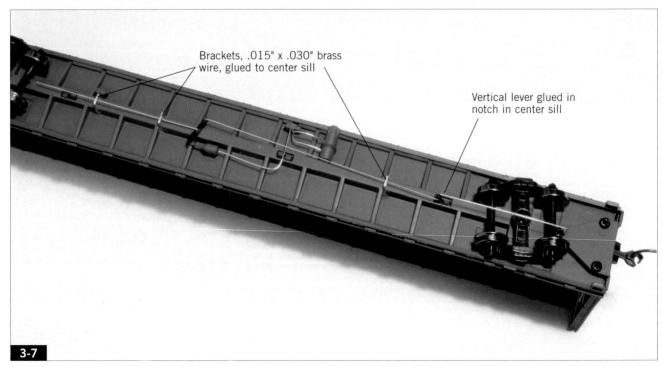

Brackets, .015" x .030" brass wire, glued to center sill

Vertical lever glued in notch in center sill

3-7

Drill the components and add wire piping, levers, and rods as with the boxcar.

3-8

The rod from the brake lever to the cylinder is exposed along the side of long piggyback flatcars.

3-9

The cylinder, valve, and reservoir are prominent, as they hang below the side sill.

Again, this car doesn't have all of the parts of the real thing, but it has enough to provide a good representation of the prototype car. You can see the completed car on page 83.

Piggyback flatcar

Long piggyback flatcars show a lot of brake gear, including the long brake rod running from the brake lever to the cylinder, **3-8** and **3-9**. Here is a pair of upgraded HO cars: the Accurail 89-foot all-purpose flatcar and the Walthers 89-foot C-channel-side car.

Start with the brake rod. Drill a no. 80 hole behind the bottom of the brake lever post, **3-10**, and glue a small piece of .012" wire in the hole. Glue the end link of a scale 28" length of 40 links-per-inch chain (such as A-Line no. 29219) to the wire.

Make three brackets from .015" x .030" brass strip (Detail Associates no. 2524), bending them to shape with fine needle-nose pliers. Glue them in place inside the side sill. This provides a guide for the .010" rod, **3-11**.

Glue another small piece of wire in the end of the cylinder piston, **3-11**, and attach a scale 40" length of chain to it. Cut the brake rod from .010" brass wire, long enough so that the chain will be slack on each end. Bend the tip of each end and slip the rod through the brackets. Glue the chain to the bent tip at each end and glue the rod to one of the brackets with a light touch of CA.

Add piping from the cylinder to the valve, **3-11**. Glue a retainer valve from a Cal-Scale brake set into a piece of Evergreen .100" styrene channel and glue it in place inside the side sill.

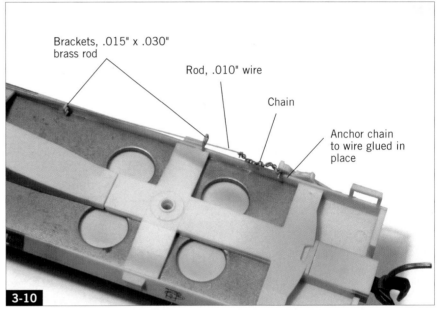

Brackets, .015" x .030" brass rod

Rod, .010" wire

Chain

Anchor chain to wire glued in place

3-10

Glue the brackets in place, then add the rod and connect it with chain to the rear of the lever molding.

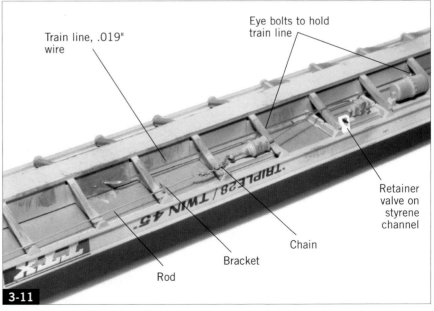

Train line, .019" wire

Eye bolts to hold train line

Chain

Retainer valve on styrene channel

Bracket

Rod

3-11

Connect the rod to the piston with chain and then add the train line, retainer valve, and piping.

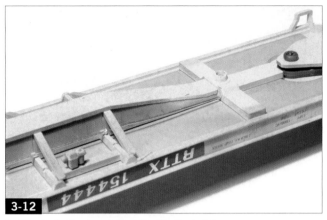

3-12

End the train line in a hole drilled in the bolster.

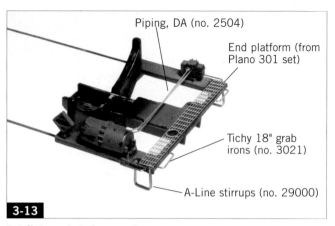

Piping, DA (no. 2504)

End platform (from Plano 301 set)

Tichy 18" grab irons (no. 3021)

A-Line stirrups (no. 29000)

3-13

Detail the end platform as shown.

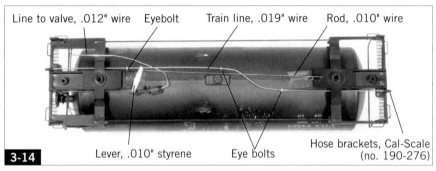

Line to valve, .012" wire   Eyebolt   Train line, .019" wire   Rod, .010" wire

Lever, .010" styrene   Eye bolts   Hose brackets, Cal-Scale (no. 190-276)

3-14

Add the train line, lever, and rods.

3-15

Hold the train line in place with eye bolts. Drill no. 80 holes for the bolts.

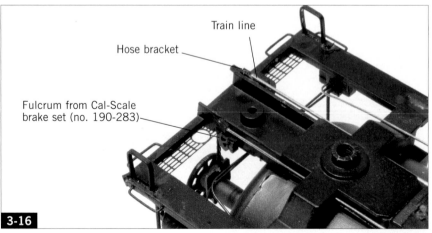

Train line

Hose bracket

Fulcrum from Cal-Scale brake set (no. 190-283)

3-16

The fulcrum is glued to the side of the draft-gear box, with the rod from the lever going into a hole drilled in the fulcrum.

The train line runs along the cross bearers next to the center sill. Glue eye bolts in place on several cross pieces to hold the line and drill a no. 61 hole into the center sill for the train line where it crosses to the other side of the car. Continue the train line on the other side of the car in the same manner. End the train line in the bolster to hide it from view, **3-12**.

Paint the new components yellow, add some weathering, and the car is much closer to its prototype as photos **3-8** and **3-9** show. Chapter 4 shows the car after more details have been added.

Tank car

Much of the brake gear on real tank cars – especially those of the modern frameless design – is in the open, but many tank car models leave it to the imagination. Walthers makes a realistic HO model of a Funnel-Flow car (one with both ends of the tank sloping toward the middle), but the model's lack of brake rigging is immediately apparent.

I added new grab irons and sill steps as well as an etched running board to the end platforms (more on such details in chapter 4). For the brake gear, drill the brake valve, cylinder, and reservoir as with the other cars shown earlier. The valve and reservoir are on the B (brake) end platform, so add the pipe lines between the two, **3-13**, test-fitting the tank to make sure the piping clears the tank. Glue the tank to the platforms.

The train line is quite visible on these cars. Model it with .019" wire, bent to shape, **3-14**, and hold it in place with eye bolts, **3-15**. When the fit is correct, glue the bolts in place.

The ends of the train line fit into the ends of Cal-Scale air hose brackets (no. 276), **3-14** and **3-16**. Add the pipe to the brake cylinder, then glue a lever in place at the end of the cylinder piston, along with the brake rods to each end. Make sure all of these parts clear the trucks.

Prepare the brake fulcrum (from the Cal-Scale brake set) by drilling out the rod connection point, **3-17**. This provides a secure connection point to the rod, **3-16**. Glue the fulcrum to the side of the coupler box so that the vertical shaft fits under the brake wheel housing.

Paint these detail items to match the car. The car still needed some final painting, weathering, and decals, which are applied in chapter 6, where you can see a photo of the finished car on page 60.

Covered hopper

Covered and open hopper cars also reveal brake gear, mostly on the ends. Some models include this rigging; others include just the cylinder, reservoir, and valve, and perhaps the brake lever.

You can make such models more realistic by adding piping, as the Walthers HO car in **3-18** shows. The biggest challenge of these cars is getting into the tight space, so disassemble the car as much as possible to drill holes and install the wire.

Another distinctive item on covered hoppers is the train line. This generally runs under one of the sides, **3-19**, to keep it outside the hopper bays. Model this with brass wire, held in place with eye bolts. If you add air hoses to the car, you can run the wire all the way to air-hose brackets next to the coupler boxes; you can also simply dead-end the wire out of sight under the ends.

Train-line placement varied with manufacturer and car style on prototype cars; some had the pipe on the left side, some on the right – check prototype photos for reference. The finished Burlington car is shown on page 68.

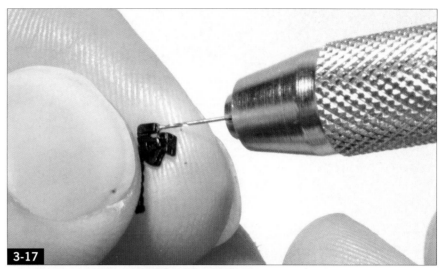
3-17
Carefully drill out the rod end of the fulcrum with a no. 80 bit. Give the bit a starting point by pressing the center of the area with a straight pin.

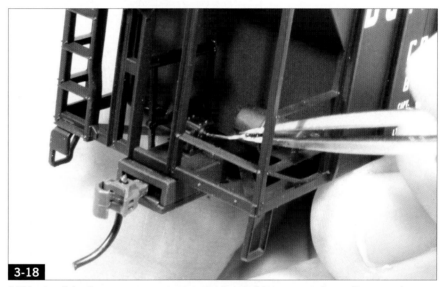
3-18
Add brake piping between components on the B end of hopper cars. Depending upon the mounting, you might be able to do some of this with the car disassembled.

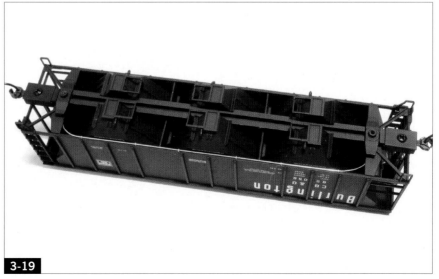
3-19
The train line on covered hoppers generally runs along one side to allow clearance.

CHAPTER FOUR

Body details

Upgrading and adding details such as sill steps, brake gear, an uncoupling lever, a running board, and a brake wheel have made this HO Accurail model much more realistic.

Many models represent essential freight car safety appliances and other details well, but others omit some of these components or have heavy, oversize details. Adding or upgrading even a few of these components will give you a more accurate, realistic model. Let's start by looking at some details that can be found on almost every car.

Air hoses

Air hoses are a continuation of the brake system discussed in chapter 3. Glad hands, cast-metal connectors at the end of each hose, allow them to be connected between cars, providing a continuation of the train line. As you look at a car end, the hose is on the right side of the coupler.

Some models come equipped with hoses, and detail parts are available in HO and N from several manufacturers. The Cal-Scale HO version, **4-1** (no. 276), includes a separate mounting bracket. The bracket is first glued in place next to the coupler box, then the hose is glued to the bracket. The train line piping (if you choose to add it) connects to the other end of the bracket (see the tank car in photo **3-16**).

Although hoses are easy details to add, some modelers choose not to add them, thinking they look odd next to the large uncoupling pins on knuckle couplers. An option is to cut off the uncoupling pins and rely on manual uncoupling. This results in a better-looking car, but requires more effort in making up trains.

Once hoses are installed, paint them grimy black. You can use a fine-point brush to paint the glad hands and angle cock (the valve handle at the top of the hose) dark gray to represent metal.

Uncoupling levers

Every prototype freight car has an uncoupling lever (sometimes inaccurately called a cut lever or lift bar) on each end. They're on opposite corners, on the left as you're looking at the end of the car (see page 30). Pulling the end of the lever pulls a pin on the coupler, opening the knuckle.

More and more models now come factory equipped with uncoupling levers, but if a model doesn't have one, they're one of the easiest details to add. Many modelers add this detail to every car before placing it in service.

In HO scale, wire versions are made by Cal-Scale and Detail Associates (DA), and Plano makes etched-brass modern levers, **4-2**. BLMA offers etched levers in N scale. Installing any of these types is usu-

4-1

Air hoses can be mounted next to the draft-gear box on the opposite side from the uncoupling lever.

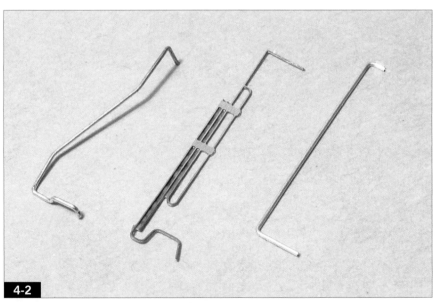

4-2

Available uncoupling levers in HO include DA no. 6215, Plano no. 12002, and DA no. 6240.

ally a matter of adding an eye bolt or bracket to the bottom corner of the car end and threading the lever through the eye bolt, **4-1**.

Since you can't attach the lever directly to the model couplers, it's usually best to glue the end of the lever to the coupler box cover with a small drop of cyanoacrylate adhesive (CA), **4-1**. If the cover needs to be removed for any reason, you can leave the lever glued in place and pull it out carefully through the eye bolt.

You'll have to adjust the placement of the eye bolt depending upon the coupler and lever. On some models,

4-3

The extended draft gear on this car required an uncoupling lever custom-formed from brass wire. Two eye bolts help hold the lever.

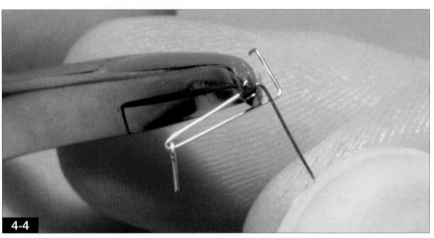

4-4

Bend the wire to shape using a small needlenose pliers.

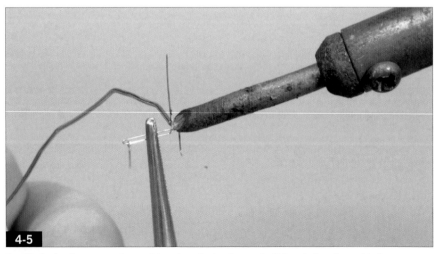

4-5

A self-closing tweezers clamped in a bench vise leaves both hands free for soldering.

you may have to add a small piece of plastic in the corner, **4-3**.

Some cars – especially those with extended cushioned draft gear – have unusual shapes and designs for uncoupling levers. You can make your own levers for these cars, bending them from .012" brass wire, **4-3**. To make a lever as I did for an HO Con-Cor reefer, start by bending the wire to shape, **4-4**. You might not be able to form a lever exactly following the prototype, but it's usually possible to make a reasonable copy.

This lever required soldering for the end of the wire that extends to the coupler. To do this, use a self-closing tweezers to hold it in place while soldering, **4-5**. Hold the soldering iron to the joint until it's hot, then touch the solder to the joint until it flows, remove the iron, and let the joint cool.

Sill steps (stirrups)

Sill steps (commonly called stirrups or stirrup steps) are located at the ends of each side of almost every car. Prototype sill steps come in a variety of styles, with straight or tapered legs, and in various widths.

Although many new models have finely molded sill steps that are quite

32

realistic, stirrups remain a visual sore spot on many models. Those that are molded in styrene with the body shell tend to be heavy and thick.

Replacement stirrups are available in several styles in HO from A-Line, Detail Associates, and others, **4-6**, and in N scale from BLMA and Gold Medal Models. Some are metal (brass and steel), others are molded in engineering plastic, and the BLMA and Gold Medal versions are etched.

Begin by cutting off the car's original steps with a sprue cutter. I wanted to replace the original steps on the Accurail boxcar on page 30 with ones that matched the prototype. Clean the area if necessary with a hobby knife or needle file. Determine the spacing of the new mounting holes by holding the new step in place and marking the location of the step mounting holes with a straight pin, **4-7**. (Some manufacturers include drilling templates with their details.) Keep the marks centered on the car side.

Use a pin vise to drill mounting holes for the steps, **4-8**. Each

Drilling templates

If you add the same detail parts to multiple cars, you can often save time by making a drilling template from thin (.010" or .020") sheet styrene. Mark the hole locations on the plastic and drill the proper diameter holes for the part. The template should align with a reference point on the car (end, sill, etc.) to make it easy to place parts.

Place the template on the car and use it to either mark the holes or as a guide for the drill bit itself.

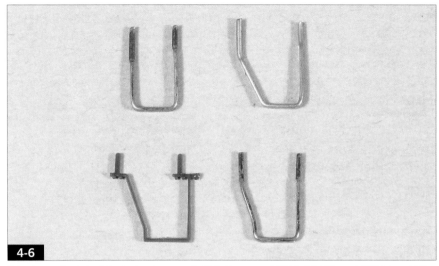

4-6

HO stirrups include (clockwise from top left) A-Line nos. 29000, 29001, and 29002 and DA no. 6411.

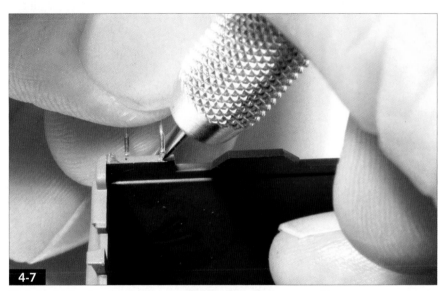

4-7

Mark the drilling locations with a pin using the new sill step as a guide.

4-8

Drill mounting holes, being sure to keep the bit straight.

4-9

Dip the ends of the new stirrup in cyanoacrylate adhesive (CA), then push them in place.

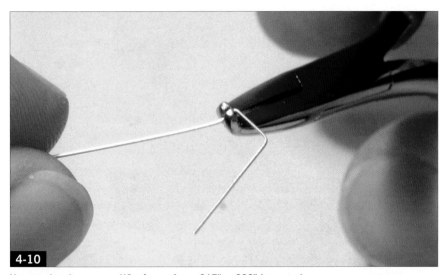

4-10

You can bend your own HO stirrups from .015" x .030" brass rod.

manufacturer's parts use different size holes – drill a test hole in scrap material if you're unsure of the proper bit to use. Keep the bit perpendicular, so it doesn't go through the car side. Drill the hole only as deep as necessary for mounting the part.

Test-fit the stirrup in place. Dip the mounting ends in a small puddle of CA on a piece of scrap plastic, then press the step in place, **4-9**. Repeat the process for the remaining steps.

Stirrups on some cars have unique or unusual shapes. You can make your own steps for these cars using thin brass wire or rod, **4-10**. For an HO Walthers 89-foot piggyback car, I used Detail Associates .015" x .030" brass rod. Use fine needlenose pliers to bend the step to shape following drawings or photos – it might take a couple of tries to get the shape just right. Once you have a good step, use it as a pattern for forming the remaining steps. Install them as with other steps, **4-11**.

Grab irons

Grab irons are also potential upgrade items on many cars, depending upon the quality of the model's originals. Prototype cars have grab irons on the ends as well as sides, and depending upon the car type and grab location, the irons will be in many lengths and styles.

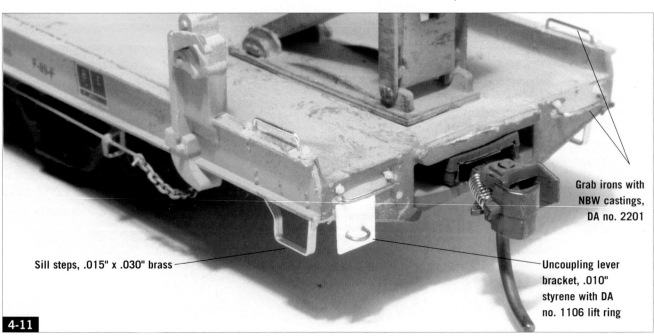

Grab irons with NBW castings, DA no. 2201

Sill steps, .015" x .030" brass

Uncoupling lever bracket, .010" styrene with DA no. 1106 lift ring

4-11

Add new sill steps and grab irons to the Walthers piggyback car.

Replacement parts are made in HO by Detail Associates, Tichy, and others, **4-12**, and in N scale from BLMA and Gold Medal. Straight and drop grab irons are generally made from brass or steel wire; bracket-style grabs are usually molded in engineering plastic. Keep a variety of styles and sizes handy.

Molded-on grab irons can be removed and replaced with separate details, but removing molded grabs from decorated models can be tricky. Depending upon the location, you can remove cast-on grabs with sprue nippers or a hobby knife. The best tool I've found for the job is Micro-Mark's detail-removing chisel (no. 82709), **4-13**.

Placing masking tape around the cast-on part helps protect the surrounding area in case the knife or chisel slips. Go slowly and don't try to remove too much material at once. On the final pass, the area should be level with the rest of the body.

Mark locations for the new grabs as with the sill steps shown earlier, then drill mounting holes for the new parts. (Templates can be handy for this; see the sidebar on page 33.) Use a fine-point brush to touch up the body color over the shaved-off part, **4-14**. You want to get the color as close as possible, but if it's not an exact match, a clear coat and a bit of weathering will help hide the area, **4-15**.

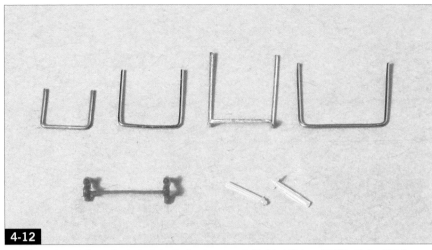

4-12

Common HO grab irons include (clockwise from top left) DA 14" (no. 2225), Tichy 18" (no. 3021), DA 18" drop-style (no. 2202), Tichy 24" (no. 3053), DA nut-bolt-washer castings (no. 2203), and DA bracket (no. 6209).

4-13

Micro-Mark's chisel works well for removing cast-on parts. Masking tape protects surrounding details and surfaces.

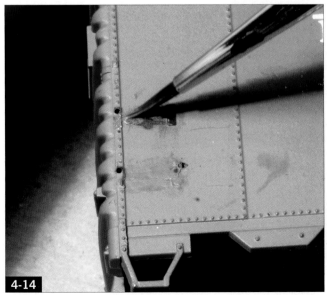

4-14

Use a brush to touch up the shaved-away area. Weathering can help cover paint that doesn't quite match.

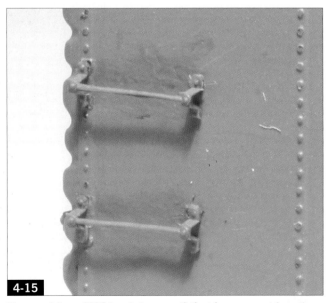

4-15

The new DA no. 6209 brackets are a distinct improvement from the molded grabs.

4-16

The new grabs and stirrups result in much finer detail on the finished car.

Top rung removed to match prototype

Ladder, DA no. 6241

Original ladder mounting holes on body – original mounting pegs glued in place and shaved smooth

Stand-offs, .010" x .030" styrene strip

4-17

Glue the new ladder in place with CA placed on the new styrene stand-offs.

Iron-type grabs are usually attached to real cars with bolts, which can be represented on models (HO and larger) with nut-bolt-washer (NBW) castings, **4-11**. To add these, drill a hole just to the side of each end of the grab iron and glue the NBW casting in place. The effect looks good on the finished car, **4-16**.

Ladders

More and more HO cars now come equipped with separate, rather than molded-on, side and end ladders. Ladder styles are a good spotting feature on prototype boxcars and reefers – for example, both seven- and eight-rung ladders were used on AAR boxcars.

Several manufacturers offer ladders for modern and steam-era cars. For kits with separate details, ladders are a fairly easy substitution. Most kits have locating pins on the backs of ladders that match holes on the body. With replacement parts, these often won't line up, so you may have to fill the existing mounting holes on the body and drill new holes. Body putty or a small drop of CA works for this. You can also cut off the original ladder pins, glue them in place on the car, and shave the area smooth, as I did on the car in **4-17**.

Instead of using the mounting pins on the back of the new ladder, it's often easier to get precise alignment (and a

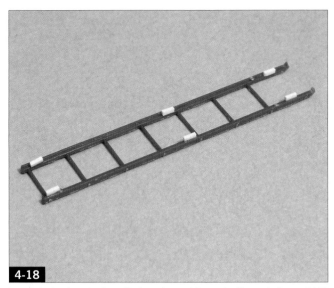

4-18

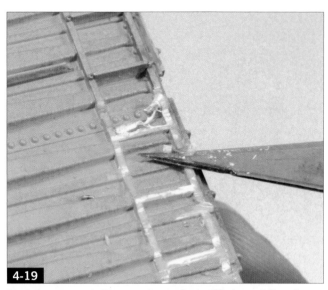

4-19

Instead of using the installation pins, add stand-offs made from .010" x .030" styrene strip.

Removing cast-on ladders requires patience. Work carefully to keep the shape of underlying details, such as end ribs.

better appearance) by making stand-offs from plastic. Cut scale 6"-long pieces of .010" x .030" styrene strip and glue them to the ladder with CA, **4-18**. Once the glue dries, use a wire to add CA to each of the new "mounting pads." Then carefully position the ladder on the car and press it in place, **4-17**.

Removing cast-on ladders is more difficult than grabs, as underlying details such as end rivet strips or car-end corrugations often interfere. I lowered the molded-on end ladders on a Con-Cor HO refrigerator car using both a hobby knife, **4-19**, and a Micro-Mark chisel. I then repainted the end, **4-20**.

There's no single magic technique for improving ladder detail – be patient, work slowly, and try to follow the contours of the end corrugations as you remove material. If the proper style of end is available as a separate item, it's probably easier to replace the entire end (more on that in the next chapter).

Brake wheels

Although small, brake wheels are a distinctive spotting feature on freight cars. Until the 1960s, when manufacturers settled on a common design, each maker's brake wheel featured a unique design, **4-21**. Kadee offers a wide variety of sharply detailed brake wheels in HO scale, and other manufacturers offer brake wheels along with brake housings.

4-20

The top of the cast-on end ladder has been removed and the end repainted.

4-21

Replacement HO brake wheels include (clockwise from top left) Kadee Modern (no. 2025), Kadee Champion (no. 2024), DA Miner (no. 6402), Kadee Ajax (no. 2020), Kadee Equipco (no. 2021), and Kadee Universal (no. 2023).

4-22

The original Accurail brake wheel isn't very realistic.

4-23

Substituting a Kadee wheel makes a big difference.

4-24

An AEI tag can be found on the right car side of all modern freight cars.

Some stock brake wheels are rather heavy or crude, **4-22**. If this is the case, or if you know that a model has the incorrect style of wheel, replace it with a new one. I used a Kadee no. 2020 Ajax wheel to match a Burlington prototype, **4-23**.

You can sometimes use the same mounting hole for a new brake wheel, but if the replacement's shaft is smaller in diameter, fill the hole with putty (or glue the shaft from the old wheel in place) and re-drill it for the new wheel.

AEI tags

An often-overlooked detail on models of modern cars, Automatic Equipment Identification (AEI) tags have been standard on all prototype freight cars since 1994, **4-24**. A-Line and Detail Associates offer these parts, which are simple to install. Simply drill a mounting hole on the car and glue it in place (see models on pages 54 and 57).

Real AEI tags use passive radio signals that provide car data to trackside scanners. The tag is located on the right of each car side above the truck. Placement varies by car type – look at prototype cars (or photos) for examples. They are generally gray but are sometimes painted to match the car.

Additional details

The best way to find details for upgrading your freight cars is to study photos or look at the real thing. With all of the available parts and a little bit of handiwork, you can take the level of detailing on your models as far as you want.

Left, right, A, B

The four sides of a prototype car are identified by their orientation to the brake end of the car, that is, the end with the brake wheel. This end is the B end (think "B" for brake); the opposite (non-brake) end is the A end. The left and right sides are identified by their location as you stand looking at the B end of a car. Boxcars sometimes have small "L" and "R" markings near the doors on each side.

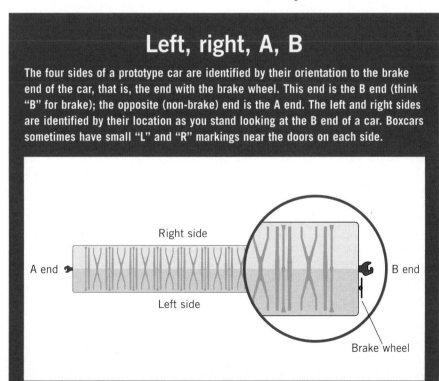

CHAPTER FIVE

Modifying cars

Adding a see-through screen to the side of this HO scale refrigerator car makes it look much more like the real thing. There are many opportunities to modify freight cars to make them more realistic.

Chapter 4 covered basic detail improvements for freight cars, but there are many more ways of upgrading rolling stock if you're willing to cut some plastic. Some of these modifications are car- or era-specific; others apply to a wide variety of cars.

5-1

Six-foot HO doors are available in an early Youngstown design from InterMountain, late Youngstown from Red Caboose, and Superior-style seven- and five-panel doors from Accurail.

Boxcar doors

The 40-foot boxcar was the most common prototype car through the steam and early diesel eras, and for many modelers, these boxcars make up a majority of their fleets. Although these (and later 50-foot) cars all look similar at first glance, many variations existed among them. Key spotting features include the ends, roofs, running boards, and doors.

Among the easiest – and most noticeable – variations you can capture on a boxcar is the side door. Many companies offer doors as separate detail items, and many manufacturers include multiple door types in their kits. Be sure to keep extras for future use. The size is critical: Early boxcars had six-foot-wide openings, with later cars having seven- and eight-foot openings. The height also varied, as early steel boxcars had a 10'-0" inside height, which later increased to 10'-6".

Steel doors came in several types, with Youngstown and Superior the two most common. Youngstown (or Youngstown-Camel, since Camel supplied the hardware) doors were the most commonly used, **5-1**. These doors can be identified by their horizontal corrugations in three panels. Early Youngstown doors had recessed panel joints and the door-lift handle was on the left side at the bottom; later Youngstown doors had raised panel separations, and the handle was at the center of the bottom of the door.

Superior panel doors are nearly flat with several horizontal stiffeners. They are identified by the number of panels, with five- and seven-panel doors the most common.

Pullman-Standard offered its own door design as an option on its PS-1 cars. These doors resemble Superior doors, but with raised panels. Camel doors were common on early steel boxcars and resembled Superior doors but with three panels, as on the Chicago Great Western Car on page 69.

Replacing doors

Doors are separate items in most ready-to-run and kit boxcars, making replacement a relatively easy process. Some manufacturers, notably Inter-Mountain and Kadee, design tabs on the back of doors to allow them to slide open. Adding another manufacturer's door usually means trimming off the tabs and gluing the door into place.

You can also replace molded-in doors, as on Accurail's 40-foot AAR boxcar kits. As an example, the Chicago, Burlington & Quincy had several boxcars that, although close to this model, had Superior doors instead of the Youngstown doors molded on the model.

I modified a decorated version of this model with a new Superior five-panel door (Accurail no. 113) by first removing the existing door. I drilled several holes around the perimeter of the door, **5-2**. A ⅛" to 3/16" bit works well; with larger drills it's harder to

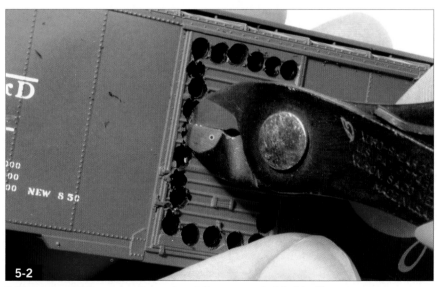

5-2

Drilling several holes makes it easy to cut the waste material with side cutters.

Use a hobby knife for the final trimming. Be careful not to remove too much material.

A motor tool with a router bit can be handy for removing material.

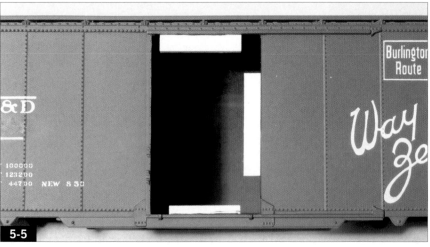

Frame the opening with strip styrene to provide a base for the new door.

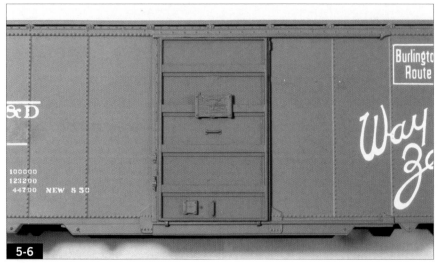

Paint the new door, then glue it in place.

control the bit. A small drill press makes the process go quickly. Be sure to use slow speed to avoid melting or tearing the plastic.

Use a sprue cutter or side cutter to trim material between the holes, **5-2**. Trim the remaining plastic to the edge of the opening with a hobby knife, **5-3**. It's important to have a sharp blade, work slowly, and not cut into the door side post or the door tracks. You can also use a routing bit in a motor tool, **5-4**. Use low speed and work slowly.

Once the opening is done, add pieces of strip styrene around the edges to give the new door a base for gluing, **5-5**. If you're modifying a decorated model, paint the new door to match the existing scheme before gluing the door in place, **5-6**.

The same methods work for modern boxcars as well. Be sure to match doors with the proper height and width. Use prototype photos or drawings as reference.

Ends and roofs

Replacing freight car ends and roofs can be trickier, as they're molded in place on many cars. Several manufacturers, including Branchline, Inter-Mountain, and Red Caboose, make separate components. The most common roofs on 40- and 50-foot AAR boxcars were the straight-panel design (often called the Murphy panel), used from the early 1930s to the mid-1940s, and diagonal panel, used from 1948 on, **5-7**. Pullman-Standard had its own roof design on its PS-1 boxcars, **5-7**. Other boxcar roofs common on wood and early steel cars included the flat seam, Hutchins, and Viking, **5-8**.

Modern boxcar roofs include variations of the diagonal panel as well as X-panel, **5-9**, and Pullman-Standard's modernized roof. Some modern boxcar roofs are peaked, but others are flat.

Boxcar ends have evolved significantly over the years. The first popular steel end was the Murphy, **5-10**, with narrow horizontal corrugations. Rib patterns on ends are generally counted on panels from top to bottom. The most common Murphy patterns were a 7/8 (shown) and a 5/5/5.

Dreadnaught ends, made by the Standard Railway Equipment Co. (later Stanray) became the dominant style in the 1930s. These ends have wider corrugations and are again identified by their pattern from top down. Cars built to the 1932 AAR design usually had 4/4 pattern ends, with square corner posts. Cars built to the 1937 AAR design were taller and used 4/5 pattern ends, **5-11**. During this

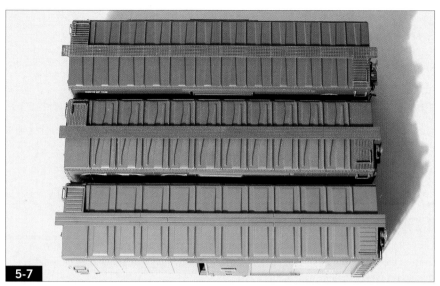

5-7

Common boxcar roofs include, from top, Pullman-Standard's PS-1 (on a Kadee car), diagonal panel (on an InterMountain car), and straight panel (on an InterMountain car).

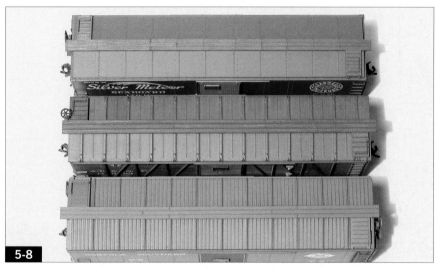

5-8

Additional roofs include flat-seam (on a Red Caboose X-29 car), Hutchins (on an Accurail single-sheathed wood car), and Viking (on a Red Caboose car).

5-10

Murphy ends, as on this Accurail HO car, were popular on wood and early steel cars.

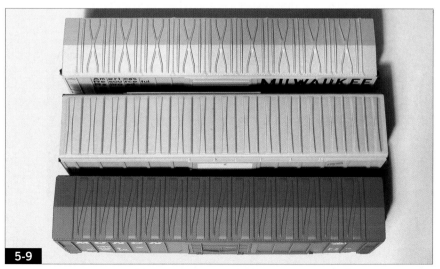

5-9

Modern boxcar roofs include the X-panel (on an Athearn Sieco car), modern PS-1 (on an Athearn PS 5344 car), and diagonal panel (on an Accurail exterior-post car).

5-11

Early Dreadnaught ends, left, have wide tapered corrugations with small "darts" between them at the sides. The PS-1 end, right, has wider corrugations that are shaped differently than those on the Dreadnaught end.

5-12

Branchline offers several Dreadnaught ends in HO, including (clockwise from top left) the 4/4 improved (no. 100004), 1/3/4 improved (no. 100001), late 1/3/4 improved (no. 100002), and "Dartnaught" (no. 100003).

5-13

Modern ends include the Stanray Dreadnaught (left, on an Athearn Sieco boxcar) and a non-terminating corrugated end (on an Athearn PS 5344 car).

time, the corner design changed from a sharp corner to a rounded design, caused by a change to internal W-shaped corner posts. These early ends had small "darts" between the tapered corrugation ends.

The 1940s saw the introduction of improved Dreadnaught ends, which replaced the small darts with long slender corrugations between the wider corrugations, **5-12**. This style continued to evolve, with changes to the shape of the corrugations (and one version without the narrow corrugations, called "Dartnaught" ends by modelers).

Pullman-Standard used ends of its own design on its PS-1 boxcars, **5-11**.

Some modern boxcars have updated versions of Dreadnaught ends; others have non-terminating ends, where the sides overlap the square corrugations on the ends, **5-13**. Spotting features include the number and size of the corrugations.

Changing ends on models is relatively easy if the parts are separate items, but it can be done even if the ends are molded in place. Start by removing the original end, **5-14**. You can remove the bulk of the end with a side cutter, then use a knife, file, or motor tool to trim away the last of the material (as with the door earlier).

Fit the new end to the body, **5-15**, and when the fit is tight, clamp and glue it in place with liquid plastic cement applied with a brush to the joints from inside. Be sure the end is the proper height for the body. Also, check to see what details are included on the end so you can determine where the end/body joint should be. For the Accurail car and Branchline end shown, the sides needed to be trimmed to the outside of the vertical rivet strip on the body, but the end of the roof ridge (which extends past that point) needed to stay on the body.

For a more complete description of boxcar (and other freight car) evolution, see the book *The Model Railroader's Guide to Freight Cars* (published by Kalmbach). Check photos of specific prototype cars to determine the proper combination of ends, roofs, doors, and other components.

5-14

Remove as much of the existing end as possible. Be alert to the amount of material and parts you'll need to leave in place on the end of the car casting.

5-15

Fit the new end to the body. This is a Branchline no. 100003 end on an Accurail AAR body.

Running boards

Running boards (not roofwalks) were required atop house cars (boxcars, reefers, and stock cars) built until 1966, **5-16**. They were made of wood into the 1940s, when galvanized steel running boards (using various patterns) became popular. Steel running boards were required on new cars starting in 1945, but wood ones could still be found on older cars through the 1960s. Laterals at diagonally opposite corners led to side ladders, with corner grab irons on the laterals. (Reefers did not have laterals, as hatches were in the way.)

Until recently, most boxcar models used injection-molded styrene pieces to simulate both steel and wood running boards. In most cases, the simulated steel parts are way too thick and don't have the see-through effect of real running boards. Wood boards molded in plastic appear shiny and lack the texture and varied appearance of the real thing.

5-16

This 1943 view shows one steel running board (foreground middle) and several cars with wood running boards in various stages of weathering. Also note the many styles of ends and roofs.

5-17

Glue styrene caps across each of the running board supports, then glue the center board in place. A bit of paint on the caps keeps any white from showing between boards.

5-18

Use cyanoacrylate adhesive (CA) to glue two brass strips in place to support the laterals.

5-19

Glue the lateral boards in place, then add the DA corner grab irons.

Wood running boards

Nothing represents wood running boards as well as wood. You can make your own from scale stripwood, or use laser-cut wood parts from American Model Builders, Modeler's Choice, or Red Caboose.

Let's start by making one from scratch. The technique I applied to an InterMountain HO boxcar will work on almost any car. Remove the original running board, saving the end running board supports if possible.

Paint enough scale 2 x 6 lumber (I used Kappler no. KP216P12) for the project (you'll need three lengths for each car). Paint the wood to match the car color; you can also stain and weather the wood to simulate the running board on an older car.

Glue caps across each of the roof's running board supports using .010" x .030" strip styrene, **5-17**. Paint the sides and ends of the caps to match the car color.

Since each car-length "board" is actually several boards long, you can either string together separate boards (keeping each butt joint over a running board support) or lay down a single board and simply scribe the joint lines with a knife or scriber. Glue the middle board in place with cyanoacrylate adhesive (CA), **5-17**, keeping it centered on the supports. Add a bit of paint on each support cap next to the board to make sure that no white plastic will show between boards.

Glue each of the outside boards in place in the same manner. The spacing doesn't have to be precise (as prototype photos show), but leave a small gap (a scale inch or two) between the outside and middle boards.

I supported the laterals on each side with .015" x .030" brass strips, **5-18**. Bend these pieces to shape, so one end wraps over the edge of the roof and the other end fits under the running board. Use CA to glue them in place.

Cut six pieces of 2 x 6 a scale 26" long and glue them to the brass strips, **5-19**, with CA making sure they overhang the brass supports enough to allow drilling holes for the corner grabs. Drill no. 80 holes for the Detail Associates no. 6205 corner grabs and

5-20

Because of the thinner diameter of its lead, a mechanical pencil works well for marking bolt locations along the planks.

5-21

The finished running board has the varied appearance of the real thing.

glue them in place. Paint the grab and exposed brass supports to match the roof and car.

With a pencil, mark bolt locations on the planks at the running board supports, **5-20**. Add the running board end supports to finish the project, **5-21**. You can save the supports from the original running board, or make your own using pieces of .020" x .030" styrene strip.

Laser-cut boards are easy to install. American Model Builders (AMB) and Red Caboose running boards and laterals are cut from a single piece of wood, **5-22**. The board separations are etched by laser, and the back has a peel-and-stick adhesive to speed installation.

To add one, remove the stock running board, again saving the end supports if possible, and add caps to the supports along the roof. Use a sharp hobby knife or razor blade to trim the AMB board from its "sprue" and test-fit it to the car. While holding the running board, bend the laterals down until they lightly snap – this will give them the proper angle to match the roof.

Place the board on your workbench upside down and remove the adhesive backing, being careful not to touch the sticky side. Add the two support boards along the edges of each lateral, then use tweezers to remove the backing paper from them. Turn the running board over and carefully position it over the car. Once you're certain the position is correct, begin pressing it in place on the supports.

The laterals have drilling marks for the corner grab irons – use them as guides to drill no. 80 holes at each location. Thread an eye bolt onto a corner grab and use tweezers or a fine needlenose pliers to press the grabs into place. Placing a bit of CA on each leg before inserting it will hold it securely.

5-22

The AMB no. 294 detail comes with the laterals and running board as a single piece. This car's roof has been weathered to simulate the wearing away of the roof's paint, which is explained in chapter 7.

5-23

Streaking the running board with paint followed with a black wash results in a realistic varied and weathered appearance.

5-24

Etched stainless-steel boards, such as this Plano offering, nicely capture the thin see-through look of the real thing.

5-25

Add Micro Kristal Klear to the running board supports at one end of the roof.

To represent a new car, simply paint the running board to match the car color. For a car that's been in service for awhile, streak the boards with the car color, then follow with a wash of grimy black or black paint, **5-23**. This gives the effect of weathered boards with peeling paint. A variation on this is to paint one board with fresh paint, making it look like repairs were recently made.

Glue the end supports – either the ones salvaged from the original board, or the parts that came with the AMB board – in place, and the running board is complete.

Steel running boards

Detail Associates (DA) and Plano both make etched stainless steel running boards (Plano in several patterns) in HO, **5-24**, and Plano and Gold Medal Models offer them in N. Kadee makes nice see-through, thin-profile engineering-plastic running boards in HO. Stainless and plastic parts each have advantages and disadvantages, but both nicely capture the look of the prototype. Prototype steel running boards were usually painted to match the car's body color, but were sometimes left their natural galvanized color.

In HO, the DA boards include the laterals in the same piece as the running board, while on the Plano boards, the laterals are separate pieces. The DA boards don't include the braces under the ends of the laterals, while Plano includes brass strips that connect the lateral to the main board.

I chose a DA running board to update my HO InterMountain car. I started by adding running board support caps across the tops of the running board supports as with the wood boards and painted them to match the car.

If you're adding the running board to an undecorated car, glue it in place before painting (unless the running board is to be left unpainted). If you're upgrading a decorated car, paint it before installing it. You'll get the best results from airbrushing; brush-painting will also work, but it takes a couple of coats, and you'll have to be careful not to fill the holes with paint.

Apply glue to two or three adjacent support caps at one end, **5-25**, and set the board in place. No glue works perfectly on stainless steel, but on the recommendations of fellow modelers, I've had good results with Microscale's Micro Kristal Klear. It holds the board securely, and when dry is less visible than CA.

Once the glue sets, lift the rest of the running board, add glue to the rest of the caps, and set the piece carefully back into place. Press the corner grabs into place in their locating holes using a small dot of CA to hold each leg in place, then add the end supports. You can also add the corner grabs before applying the board itself, securing them with CA or epoxy. The finished board has a thin profile and a realistic see-through appearance, **5-26**.

The plastic Kadee running boards have several advantages: They look good; come as a single part including end supports, laterals, and corner grabs; and are available in several colors. They're also less expensive than their steel cousins.

However, they are molded in an engineering plastic that's difficult to glue and can be tricky to install. Notches on each mounting peg are designed to lock onto slots on Kadee bodies, but this doesn't work on other manufacturers' cars.

Here's one effective method of applying them (on an Accurail boxcar as an example). Trim the mounting posts off of the laterals and trim the ends off the end supports, **5-27** (the parts that go into slots on the Kadee car).

It's difficult – if not impossible – to drill press-fit holes in precise alignment to match the Kadee running board's four mounting pegs because any deviation will cause the thin board to buckle. Instead, drill a no. 56 hole in the boxcar roof at one of the middle peg locations for a press fit, **5-28**. This will keep the board in alignment while installing it. Drill no. 54 (or larger) holes at the other peg locations, keeping the holes centered on the roof ridge. Test-fit the running board, making sure it lies flat across all of the supports, that it's centered end-to-end, and

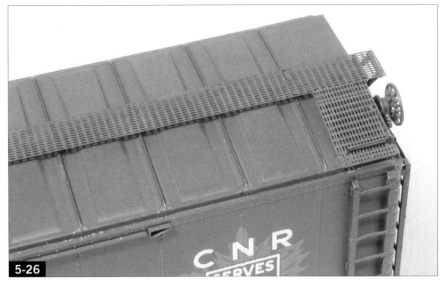

Most steel running boards were painted to match the roof; some were left in bare galvanized steel.

Trim the ends off of the end supports on the Kadee running board casting.

Drill a no. 56 hole at one peg location to hold the Kadee running board in place.

5-29

Glue a half of the running board in place at a time using CA on the running board supports.

5-30

Add body putty in the holes around each of the mounting pegs.

5-31

The finished Kadee running board has a nice see-through appearance.

that the end supports fit properly.

With the board in place, lift up one end and use a toothpick to apply CA across each running board support, **5-29**. Press the running board in place, making sure that it lies flat. Do the same with the other end.

When the glue sets, turn the car upside down and use a toothpick to work body putty into the mounting holes around the running board mounting pegs and over the pegs, **5-30**. The putty will bond to the plastic on the car, and when it hardens, it will lock onto the notch in each mounting peg, holding the running board firmly in place. The finished running board looks great, **5-31**.

The type of running board you choose is a matter of preference – try installing one of each to see how they work for you. Many modelers choose etched boards to represent unpainted boards (an airbrushing of thinned flat gray or grimy black tones down the silver and gives it a more-realistic galvanized-steel appearance), but the same modelers may prefer Kadee boards to represent prototypes that were painted.

Upgrading running boards certainly isn't limited to boxcars and reefers. Covered hoppers have prominent running boards, and replacing thick plastic originals greatly improves their appearance.

Tank car platforms, intermodal car platforms, and boxcar brake platforms have potential for upgrading with see-

5-32

The running board of this Chicago & North Western 40-foot AAR boxcar, built in 1952, was removed in 1974. The two ladders at right have been shortened to four rungs, but you can still see the mounting lugs for the tops of the ladders as well as the lugs for the removed running-board end support.

through replacements. Detail Associates, Plano, and Gold Medal offer a variety of parts for HO and N scales.

Removing running boards

If you model the period from the late 1960s to today, you'll need to accomplish the opposite of the above – you'll have to remove running boards from some cars. New cars couldn't have running boards after 1966, and at that time, running boards on older cars were scheduled to be removed by 1974 (although that date was pushed back to 1979, and a few cars still had them after that).

When removing running boards, railroads usually left the running board supports in place. The side and end ladders on the corner diagonally opposite the brake wheel were cut down to four rungs, but the mounting lugs often remained in place, **5-32**. The brake wheel was usually left in place, but it was lowered on some cars.

Modeling these transitional ladder types is a matter of cutting down the ladders (as on the reefer in chapter 4) and removing the running board. If the running board had mounting pegs, you'll need to fill the holes. Detail

Associates makes plugs for this task in HO (no. 6224), or you can fill them with body putty or thick CA.

Using CA is quick and easy; drop a little in the hole, **5-33**, then apply a drop or two of super glue accelerator to cure it. Add another drop of CA if necessary, followed by more accelerator. (Apply drops of accelerator with a toothpick or pipette to control it better than from its spray bottle.)

Smooth the area with a modeler's chisel, knife, and sanding stick or sandpaper, **5-34**, and blend it with the roof. If filling holes with CA, you need to carve and smooth within a few minutes

5-33

Add CA to the hole, then use accelerator to cure it. It may take two or three applications of CA.

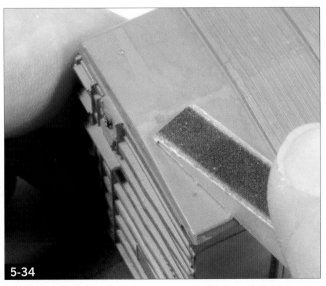

5-34

Smooth the filled area with a hobby knife, chisel, sanding stick, or fine sandpaper.

5-35

Washes of black, grimy black, and brown give the American Model Builders deck the look of individual weathered boards.

of adding accelerator or the CA will soon become too hard to shape. Add a corner grab iron directly to the roof at the brake-wheel end.

Flatcar decks

Since they're out in the open, flatcar decks draw attention. Decks on real cars are generally wood, while the decks on most models are molded in plastic. You can add a wood deck of stripwood pieces or scribed wood sheet, but several adhesive-backed laser-cut wood decks are available from AMB and others, and they're easy to install.

I used an American Model Builders deck on an HO scale Proto 2000 50-foot flatcar. The first step was removing the car's plastic deck and test-fitting

the new deck. I made sure the deck was clean and clear of dust and debris, then peeled the backing paper from the deck and pressed it in place.

Weathering is the key to a realistic wood floor. Mix a series of paint washes using Polly Scale Grimy Black, Steam Power Black, and Railroad Tie Brown (one part paint and nine parts Polly Scale Airbrush Thinner). Brush the washes on the individual boards of the deck, **5-35**, varying the colors and intensity on each board. Combine the washes on some boards to get different colors.

The finished stained wood deck looks much more like a weathered flatcar deck than the plastic original, **5-36**. You can use the same methods for gondolas with wood floors.

Mechanical refrigerator car

Mechanical refrigerator cars often have a screened opening over the diesel engine and refrigeration equipment at one end of the car, **5-37**. However, most manufacturers attempt to replicate this with molded-in detail.

You can improve the appearance of a such models by cutting out this area of the plastic and replacing it with

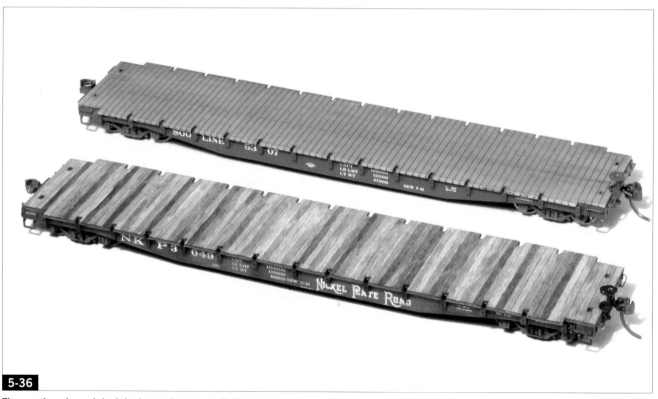

5-36

The weathered wood deck looks much more realistic than the Proto 2000 car's original plastic deck.

5-37

The screen covering the cooling equipment gives this PFE mechanical refrigerator car a distinctive appearance.

brass screen wire. Start by cutting out the screened openings on each side with the same techniques described for removing a boxcar door in chapter 4.

Once the plastic is gone, frame the opening with .020" x .030" styrene to provide a base for the new screen, **5-38**. Paint the frame to match the car – Polly Scale Reefer Orange in this case. Cut the new screen from Scale Scenics brass Micro-Mesh (no. 652-3501) and paint it grimy black. Apply CA around the frame with a small wire or toothpick, then set the screen in place. A four-rung Detail Associates ladder glued over the screen replaces the car's original molded-on ladder. Paint the interior of the car – some of which is now visible through the screen – with flat medium gray.

Since the interior is now visible, you'll want to find some gear to resemble refrigeration equipment. I used a small roof air conditioner unit from a Walthers set, **5-39**, placed on the floor at the end. Although this is by no means an accurate representation of what's inside the real car, it's close enough to give the impression of interior equipment, as the photo on page 40 shows.

Upgrade path

The projects in this chapter are only a starting point – you can give your freight cars hundreds of other potential upgrades.

5-38

Cut out the simulated screen and frame the opening with strip styrene. The new screen is Scale Scenics Micro-Mesh.

5-39

An air conditioning unit glued to the floor simulates the cooling equipment on the real car.

CHAPTER SIX

Decals and lettering

Many separate lettering items enhance this factory-painted Walthers car, including the Chemtrec label, consolidated stencil, commodity lettering, and hazardous-material placard and number plate.

Even though most freight car models today come painted and lettered – and even assembled – the many specialty decals on the market offer plenty of opportunities to further detail your freight cars. Some of these items are era-specific, allowing you to more accurately match cars to the time frame you model.

6-1

The original capacity data on this car was painted out, and the newly re-stenciled data are in a different style. Note the many chalk marks near the ends and door. Hol Wagner

Car lettering

Freight car lettering identifies the owner of the car and shows the car's unique number, among other things. Capacity and size data are important to shippers and for assigning cars to shipments. Other lettering provides information on the car's equipment and maintenance history.

Some of this lettering is optional, but much of it is mandatory, and many of these items have changed over the years. Knowing when each lettering element was required and used will help you match your cars to a specific era and will make them more realistic.

The sidebar on page 56 shows some varieties of lettering on freight cars.

Capacity data

Freight cars are periodically reweighed, especially after repairs are made. The new light weight and load limit are re-stencilled on the car, along with the date and initials of the shop doing the reweighing. (If the lettering says "NEW," then the stenciling was done when the car was built, and the date will match the car's built date.)

This is often quite apparent on older cars, as the area is painted over before the numbers are re-stenciled, **6-1**. On older cars, this fresh paint can greatly contrast with the grimy car side, and the new numbers sometimes don't follow the same style as the originals.

One of the simplest ways to model this, if your model already has shop initials and reweigh date in place, is to cover the data with masking tape before weathering it. After weathering the car, peeling away the tape reveals the clean patch, which looks like a paint/re-stencil job.

You can also accomplish this like the real thing. Start by weathering the car (see chapter 7), then brush-paint out the old data, **6-2**. Don't worry about

6-2

Paint out the original data with a brush.

6-3

Decals provide the new data, date, and shop initials.

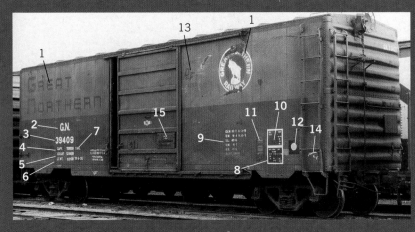

Lettering

1. **Road name and herald.**
2. **Reporting marks.** Each railroad and private owner has its own unique identifying initials; some railroads and owners have multiple marks. Reporting marks ending in "X" are privately owned.
3. **Number.** Each car has a number unique to that reporting mark.
4. **Capacity.** The car's designed capacity in pounds. Not required on cars built since 1985; often painted out on older cars.
5. **Load limit.** The maximum weight allowed for the load itself.
6. **Light weight.** The car's weight when empty.
7. **AAR mechanical code.** This is an XML boxcar, meaning a boxcar equipped with loading devices.
8. **Built date.** On modern cars this appears in the consolidated stencil.
9. **Dimensional data.** Internal and external measurements of the car; can include capacity in cubic feet (boxcars, reefers, and covered hoppers).
10. **Consolidated stencils.** (See text.)
11. **ACI plate.** (See text.)
12. **Wheel inspection dot.** (See text.)
13. **Special equipment stencil.** In this case, the car is equipped with Evans DF-2 loading devices.
14. **Chalk marks.** Chalk marks are used to convey information on trains, routing, and blocking.
15. **Tack boards.** The large wood board is the placard board; it's used for information and instructions (such as unloading). The small boards, known as route boards, are for information on car routing.

matching the original car color – railroads certainly weren't concerned about it. Add decals for the new data and the shop initials and date, **6-3**. I took mine from an old decal set; Sunshine offers a wide variety of reweigh date/initial decal sheets in HO.

Consolidated stencils

Many manufacturers offer modern cars with consolidated stencils on them, but decals allow you to update older cars, making it easier to model periods from the early 1970s to today.

Consolidated stencils first appeared in 1972 as a method of getting vital inspection information into one place on a car. You'll see various initials and dates, including COTS (clean, oil, test, and stencil for the brake system), either RPKD (repacked, for journals on solid-bearing trucks) or LUB (lubed, for roller bearings), IDT (in-date test, for brakes), RCD (reconditioned, if a car has been rebuilt), and INSP (inspected).

The first stencils were single black panels with a one-inch white border (see photo **7-5**); in 1974, two-panel consolidated stencils became mandatory on cars (with a deadline date of 1979 for application to all cars). These were sometimes adjoining but were separate on many cars. They should be located on the lower-right corner of each side, but placement didn't always follow the guidelines in the early days of stencils.

In 1982, the design changed again to four panels (three larger side-by-side panels with a narrow panel across the bottom for listing built and rebuilt dates); shortly thereafter, this was revised to three panels (two side-by-side panels with a narrow panel across the bottom). You'll find the three-panel stencils on most modern cars, but many older cars with the early two-panel separate stencils are still rolling around.

Microscale and Champ both offer decals for all styles of stencils, **6-4**. Apply these based on the period you model and the age of your car (or to match a specific prototype). I added a single-panel stencil to a refrigerator car built in the mid-1960s, **6-5**. When stencils were first added to existing

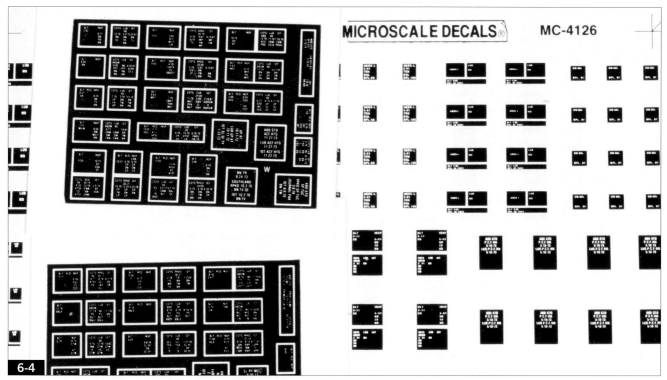

Consolidated stencil decals are made in HO by Champ (left, nos. HD-31 and HD-32) and Microscale (MC-4126).

cars, they were sometimes placed over dimensional data or other lettering.

Many flatcars don't have a large enough flat surface for a stencil, so a steel plate is welded to the side sill. This is easy to model with a piece of thin sheet styrene cut to match the stencil, **6-6**. A Microscale three-panel stencil finished the car.

ACI plates and inspection dots

Introduced in 1967, the Automatic Car Identification (ACI) system used trackside scanners to read plates with multi-colored horizontal bands on each freight car (see page 56). This automated the process of tracking car locations. All cars in interchange service were required to have ACI plates by 1970.

Grime and dirt eventually made panels unreadable to the scanners, a problem that couldn't be economically fixed, so the system was eventually dropped. Cars were no longer required to have plates after 1977, but they were usually left to weather on cars that had them (and a few cars can still be seen with some very weathered panels).

Microscale offers HO and N scale decals for ACI plates, **6-7**. If you model between 1970 and 1977, they should be on all your cars; cars built after 1977 shouldn't have them.

Wheel-inspection dots began to appear in March 1978. They were proof of inspection of a certain type of wheel that was found to be defective. Cars without the banned wheels received a black square with a yellow dot; cars with the bad wheels got a white dot and were restricted in service, with wheels to be replaced by Decem-

This refrigerator car has a consolidated stencil from Champ set no. HD-31 and a running board warning decal from Microscale set no. 87-1.

Fix a stencil decal to a styrene sheet and glue it to the side sill of a flatcar.

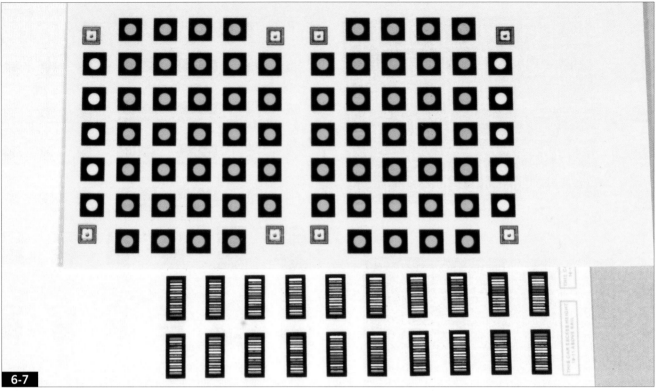

6-7

Champ set no. HD-34 includes HO wheel-inspection dots; Microscale set no. 87-2 (60-2 in N) includes ACI labels.

ber of that year. Cars built after 1980 won't have this dot.

Champion offers HO decals for dots, **6-7**, and Microscale makes them in N (60-193) and HO (87-193).

Renumbering cars

If you model a specific railroad, chances are you'll need several identical car types lettered for that railroad. For example, as a modeler of the early 1960s Chicago, Burlington & Quincy, I need several similar 40-foot boxcars lettered for the Burlington.

On real railroads, each car has its own unique number. Many model manufacturers today offer freight car models in multiple road numbers, making it easier than it used to be to have multiple cars of the same type and road name. However, on occasion you'll want multiples of the same car when only one number is offered.

Changing numbers on models can be done, with the most challenging task being removing the original number. Each manufacturer applies a different type of ink or paint for lettering, meaning a removal technique that works for one manufacturer's car might not work for another. Some lettering comes off easily; other lettering is tougher than the underlying paint.

It might be tempting to try removing and changing just one numeral, but it's usually easier in the long run to remove and replace the entire number set. The number style will be easier to match, and the end results will look much better.

I usually start with a common pencil eraser, **6-8**, protecting nearby lettering with masking tape. Rubbing the eraser across the number will sometimes do the job by itself. If that doesn't work, sometimes you can speed up the process by brushing a bit of decal-setting solution (such as Walthers Solvaset) on the number before using the eraser.

If the ink proves tougher, switch to an abrasive method. A bit of fine (600-

6-8

A pencil eraser often works well for removing factory-painted road numbers.

grit or finer) sandpaper or a sanding stick may work, or you can carefully use the edge of a hobby knife. Try to keep to the numbers and avoid working through the paint or into the body.

Occasionally it's impossible not to remove some paint along with the number. If this happens, use a fine brush to touch up the area with the body color (a hit-and-miss process – get as close a match as you can). A bit of weathering later will hide the difference in shades.

Renumber the car with a decal or dry-transfer set made for that scheme, **6-9**, or use an alphabet/number set with the closest lettering style you can find. I prefer dry transfers because the process goes quickly and there's no decal film to hide, but either will do the job.

Seal the car with a coat of clear flat finish and weather the car as desired (more on that in chapter 7).

Placards and load stenciling

Cars hauling hazardous commodities require placards listing the product code and type of material as shown in the sidebar on page 60. These are most

6-9 Use decals from a matching set to add the new road number.

common on tank cars, which haul a variety of hazardous materials such as chemicals and fuel, but placards can also occasionally be found on covered hoppers and boxcars. Tank cars have placard holders on each side and end.

Since the mid-1980s, hazardous material placards include a four-digit number that specifies the product

being carried, and small orange panels on the car also list the number. Many of these cars also carry stenciling listing the product being carried, **6-10**.

Placards of various types have been used since the early 1900s, but early placards were more general in nature, with non-product-specific lettering such as "dangerous," "flammable" or

6-10 This tank car is placarded for molten-sulfur service, with the commodity stenciled on the side, orange decals with the commodity number, and diamond-shaped placards.

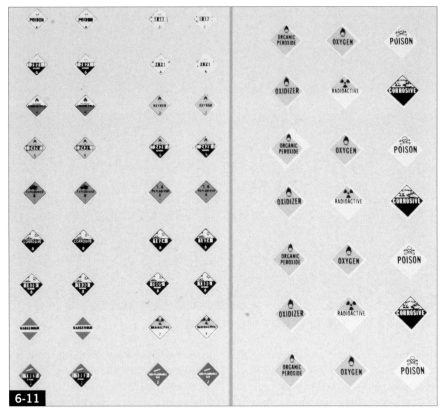

6-11

Microscale has decal sets for modern placards (left, no. 87-840) and older-style placards (no. 87-228).

"combustible." Microscale (HO and N) and Sunshine (HO) offer placards for modern and older eras, **6-11**. The design of placards has changed over the years, so check prototype photos for usage guidelines for the era you model.

Another modern piece of lettering is the Chemtrec decal, featuring black lettering on a yellow background. These began appearing on tank cars carrying hazardous materials in the 1980s. I added a label to the car in

6-12 from an Islington Station decal set for sulfur cars (no. 100-119), which is where the orange commodity labels came from as well. The diamond placards are from Microscale set no. 4126.

6-12

Decals and weathering leave no doubt that this Walthers HO scale car is carrying molten sulfur.

Commodity stenciling can be added to tank cars using dry-transfer or decal lettering. I selected a Clover House alphabet set to letter the sulfur car, **6-13**. It looks difficult, but it goes quickly, and looks great. Transfer the letters using a burnishing tool or pencil, then seal the car with a coat of clear flat or satin.

Other lettering

Chalk marks appear often on cars, **6-1**. Agents scribble on information on routing and track or train assignments, and such marks usually appear at the bottom corners of cars or next to the doors, within easy reach of a person standing on the ground.

Sunshine offers several decal sets for these scribblings in HO, **6-14**, and Microscale and others include them on some sets. Since chalk marks fade rapidly after they're applied, you can add several in layers: Add a couple, weather over them and add a clear-coat, then add more. Repeat the process as often as needed.

End lettering indicates car equipment, such as the type of wheels and the spring package (or the spring travel distance). Sunshine makes several sets of these in HO, and you can see them on a car in photo **7-13**.

Placard boards often have notes tacked to them regarding the car load, unloading instructions, or handling information. You can make these yourself using a computer and printer or use preprinted ones. Jaeger makes two sets of cards in HO scale (nos. 2100, 2150) with messages such as "do not hump" and "unload this side." Simply cut one out and glue it to the tack board, **6-15**.

Another common label began appearing in the late 1960s as running boards were removed from cars. On these cars, a "keep off roof – no running board" label was required next to the side ladder at the brake wheel end, **6-4**.

Other decal upgrade ideas include reflective dots and stripes, builder's insignia, special equipment markings, and special dedicated-service lettering. Keep your eyes open for other opportunities to add additional lettering to your freight cars.

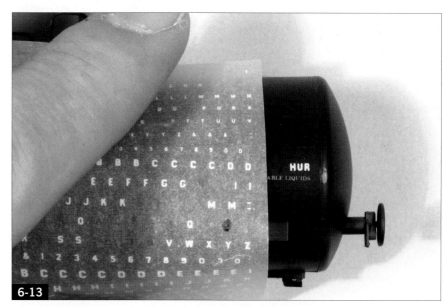
6-13 Apply individual dry transfer letters by burnishing them from the backing paper with a pencil.

6-14 Chalk-mark scribbles give model cars a unique and well-used look.

6-15 Jaeger makes several tags for placard boards.

CHAPTER SEVEN

Weathering

Weathering your cars gives them the realistic appearance of hard-working rolling stock that has been earning its keep on your railroad.

Models are clean and shiny as they come from the box, but real freight cars don't stay clean for long. Unlike passenger cars, freight cars don't get washed, and they generally don't even get a fresh coat of paint unless they've undergone major repairs. Duplicating the appearance of rust, grime, peeling paint, and other effects helps models look more like the real thing.

Variety is the key

Freight cars weather in many ways, depending upon their color, age, areas traveled, and loads. Different types and brands of paint weather differently – some fade, some peel, and some get chalky. Some old cars are just basically grimy; others have seemingly random rust patches and streaks. To obtain realistic results, look at real-life examples and photos and use a variety of techniques to capture those appearances.

Drybrushing, washes, and oversprays

There are three main ways to apply weathering with paint: drybrushing, washes, and airbrushing.

Drybrushing is easy and can create many effects. It's a good use for old brushes that aren't good for finish work anymore. To start, dip just the tip of the bristles in paint, then wipe off most of the paint on a paper towel. Streak the model with the almost-dry brush, **7-1**.

You can drybrush to simulate rust or exhaust streaks, or you can streak the car color over lettering to simulate

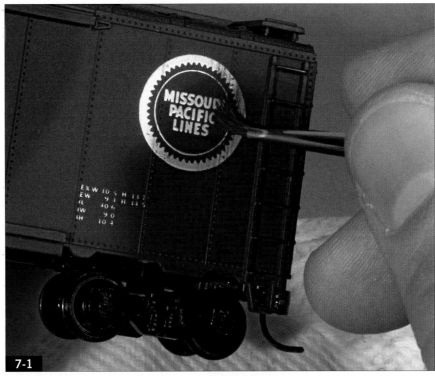

7-1

After wiping off most of the paint from a brush on a paper towel, drag the bush carefully over the model. Using the car color gives the effect of peeling, streaked lettering.

peeling paint. When working on car sides, keep most of your streaks vertical to mimic the way mother nature treats real cars.

7-2

Thin washes tend to cling around raised details such as rivets, door hardware, and vertical posts.

Washes work well on textured surfaces. To make a wash, mix one part paint with eight or nine parts thinner. For Polly Scale paints, use Polly S Airbrush Thinner; for Modelflex paints, use distilled water. You can use washes to create general grime effects on car sides, **7-2**. Washes also work well for staining wood, as shown on the flatcar deck in chapter 5.

If you have an airbrush, thinned weathering sprays can capture many effects, including exhaust effects, general grime, and rust. Thin paint in the same manner as washes.

Floquil sells mixing bottles that come in handy for holding thinned paint mixes. Old film canisters (especially the clear ones) also work well. It's a good idea to only mix as much as you plan to use in a few days, because thinned paint tends to separate.

Oil paint rust

Artist's oil paints are great for duplicating rust patches and streaks on freight cars, and thinned oil paints make excellent washes on freight car sides. The technique is flexible and provides ample working time compared to acrylic paints.

7-3

Touch the bristles of a thinner-filled brush to your palette of rust-color oil paints, then apply it down the car side.

7-4

Use a fine-point brush to apply oil color rust patches to models.

By mixing burnt umber, burnt sienna, and raw umber, you can achieve almost any color of rust, from deep brown to medium brown and light orange-brown. Squeeze a bit of each color from the tube onto a piece of scrap plastic as a palette. Mix some of the colors to get a variety of shades. The paint will remain workable for hours (days, with larger amounts of paint).

To make a wash, put a small amount of mineral spirits in a small container (I use an old film canister). Dip a flat, wide brush into the thinner, then touch the tips of the bristles on paint from your palette. Stroke the brush down the car side, **7-3**. If the initial effect is too heavy, wipe off the bristles, load the brush with more thinner, and go over the side again. Keep working until you have the effect you're looking for.

In addition to rust, you can easily create grime effects by using washes of black. Try mixing several colors for more varied effects, as in the Monon boxcar on page 62.

To simulate the rust patches that appear on many cars, use a fine-point brush to paint the oil colors on the car sides, **7-4**. I followed a pattern from a prototype covered hopper, **7-5**. After you've painted the rust patches, apply a light wash of mineral spirits with a wide brush. Letting the paint dry before streaking it results in lighter

7-5

The paint and lettering on this Burlington Northern covered hopper have peeled in many places, with rust patches showing through.

7-6

The oil paint patches and streaks on this HO Athearn model nicely capture the appearance of the prototype car.

effects; streaking it immediately after painting removes more of the patches.

Once you're satisfied with the results, set the car aside for a few days until the paint is thoroughly dry. You can then seal it with a coat of clear satin or flat finish or add additional effects with chalks or other paints, **7-6**.

Chalks

Powdered chalk replicates many types of weathering, especially overall dusty, grimy effects on car sides, roofs, and underbodies. For chalks to work well, you have to follow a few basic guidelines:

First, always apply chalks to dead-flat finishes. Chalk won't stick well to a glossy surface, and even if some stays in place, it will vanish as soon as you try to seal it with a clear coat.

Second, always use good chalk. Avoid kids' playground chalk – instead, use artist's pastel chalks, which are available in a variety of earth and rust tones. Scrape it with a hobby knife to make a powder (those always-handy film canisters are good for storing it). If you don't want to make your own, some companies, including AIM Products, **7-7**, offer weathering chalk.

Third, always seal your chalk weathering with a final clear coat. Unsealed chalk is easy to accidentally wipe off when handling, and it will show oily or sweaty fingerprints from handling.

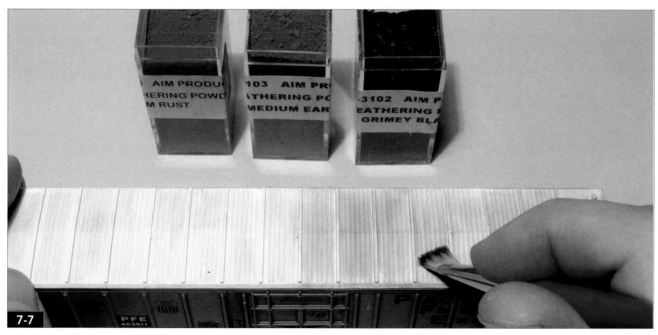

7-7

Chalks work well for overall grime and rust effects, such as on this white refrigerator car roof.

7-8

Paint trucks with a mix of black, grimy black, brown, and rust.

although some (notably Kadee) are cast metal, and a few are brass. In any case, raw plastic or unpainted metal doesn't resemble a real truck.

Prototype trucks are usually painted black, although some are painted to match the car color (usually a shade of boxcar red or brown). After a few years of service, these usually morph to a grimy black or dark gray, often with streaks or rust. Vary the level of weathering among cars, based on the age of the car.

Painting trucks goes quickly if you do it in batches. Place a few drops of black, dark brown, and rust paint on a piece of scrap plastic, **7-8**. Dab the colors with a brush, then paint the sideframes, making sure all surfaces are covered. Blending the colors with your brush on the palette yields a wide variety of colors.

A couple of details merit attention. The roller-bearing adapter (the housing directly above each roller-bearing end cap) on roller-bearing trucks is usually dark red – this is easy to highlight using a fine-point brush, **7-9**.

On solid-bearing trucks, the journal box cover and the journal just below

Let's apply these techniques to capture some prototype weathering effects.

Trucks and wheels

When weathering cars, it's a good idea to start at the bottom. Prototype wheels and trucks don't stay clean for long, as wheels kick up dirt and debris,

and rust begins forming on the metal surfaces (see the prototype trucks in chapter 2). You'll go a long way toward realism by painting all of your trucks and wheelsets before placing cars in service.

Most truck sideframes are molded in black styrene or engineering plastic,

7-9

Paint the roller-bearing adapter dark red or brown. The wheels on roller-bearing trucks don't have an oily appearance.

7-10

Oil from journal boxes gives wheels on solid-bearing trucks a greasy, textured appearance.

and around the cover are often stained with oil. Highlight these areas on some trucks with a bit of oily black paint (see the model on page 8).

Real wheels are unpainted, making it easier to check for defects. Model wheels are either plastic or metal, and even blackened metal wheels are generally too shiny to be realistic. You can use a palette of colors to paint wheels just as with truck sideframes.

Be aware that wheels weather differently on roller-bearing and solid-bearing trucks. Most wheel faces start out a fairly uniform brown to dark-orange, although some are lighter. Wheel faces on solid-bearing trucks eventually become coated with oil from the journal boxes, so older wheels tend to be darker and shiny black. In extreme cases, wheel faces become textured with grime collected by the oil, **7-10**.

Roller-bearing trucks lack this journal-box oil, so the faces generally keep their dull rust color. They may darken over time and sometimes have a dull grimy cast (see photos **2-3**, **6-10**, and **7-5**).

To capture the texture of an old, greasy wheel face, start by painting the face with black paint. While the paint is still wet, sprinkle powdered chalk on the face and press it in place, **7-11**. Let it dry for several minutes, then use a

7-11

Press powdered chalk into the wet black paint on the wheel face.

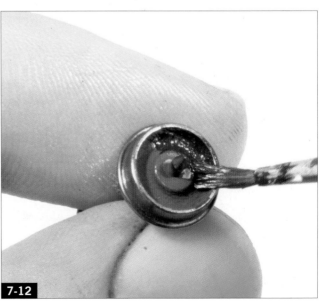

7-12

Paint the now-textured wheel face with Polly Scale Oily Black paint.

7-13

Paint couplers shades of brown and rust and paint air hoses and/or uncoupling pins grimy black.

stiff brush to remove the excess chalk. Finish the wheel, **7-12**, by giving it a light coat of Polly Scale Oily Black paint (you can mix it with gloss black to vary the appearance). See the finished truck on page 8.

Wheel treads on real cars are shiny from wear. However, don't forget to paint the wheel backs and axles – any shade of dark brown or dark rust will do nicely. The rims (outside edges, visible from the sides) are sometimes grimy, but can also be shiny – wheel retarders in hump yards grab the rims to slow cars down, polishing them in the process.

Couplers

Prototype couplers are also unpainted, meaning most are some shade of rust or brown. Paint the couplers on your

7-14

Use a white or light gray artist's crayon to lightly trace the bottoms of the letters on the car side.

7-15

A stiff brush streaks the marks from the artist's crayon down the side.

7-16

Add additional weathering as desired to complete the car. This is a Walthers HO model.

models on the sides and top, but be aware that any paint on or inside the knuckle will wear off with use, **7-13**.

Many knuckle springs are an unrealistic bright bronze color, so be sure to paint them to kill the color. A shot of thinned dark brown or rust from your airbrush will do the trick. You can use a brush, but make sure you don't leave a lot of paint in the moving parts, as that could impede the coupler's operation.

If you leave the uncoupling pins in place, be sure to paint them black or grimy black. This helps hide them, and at least resembles the color of air hoses.

Fading lettering

As cars age, the paint from white lettering sometimes becomes chalky and streaks down the side of the car, which is especially apparent on large lettering. You can capture this look with a white or light gray artist's crayon. Lightly trace the bottoms of the letters on the car with the crayon, **7-14** – it doesn't take much!

Next, streak the letters with a stiff brush, **7-15**. (Hog bristle brushes are inexpensive and work great for this as well as for chalk weathering.) The brush will carry the crayon color down the car side, **7-16**. Be sure to move the brush directly down the sides. You can

make this effect as light or heavy as you like.

Lettering also tends to fade over time, and sometimes almost completely disappears. You can capture this effect with a pencil eraser, **7-17**, in the same manner as removing road numbers (chapter 6).

If that doesn't work, you can achieve

a similar effect by drybrushing the car color over the lettering. Finish the car with additional weathering, **7-18**.

Patching and relettering

Freight cars, just like any business asset, are bought and sold. A change in appearance for sold equipment is especially common when equipment

7-17

You can often fade lettering by streaking it with a pencil eraser.

7-18

The finished car captures the effect of real lettering that's bleached and faded from the sun.

leases run out (typically around 15 years of service) or, as with the Chicago & North Western boxcar in **7-19**, the former owner (Rock Island) goes out of business. In some cases, the new owners or lessors completely repaint cars, but many times the old cars receive a patchwork treatment. Old reporting marks are painted out and new ones added, or new owners may paint out the old logos, road names, and reporting marks, as did the C&NW.

You can duplicate this effect by doing just what the real railroad does. I started with an HO Athearn boxcar lettered for the Rock Island. Start by weathering the car (lightly in this case, since the Rock folded just two years after buying these cars).

Paint over the old lettering with a brush using a shade that doesn't quite match the car's original color. I grabbed whatever blue was handy.

Then you need to add new lettering. For my car, Microscale makes a set for the Chicago & North Western's relettered cars (no. 87-259), including reporting marks, number, and herald. Finish by weathering, **7-20**, to taste.

Car roofs

From trackside it's difficult to see the tops of real freight cars, but the viewpoint of our layouts makes the roofs of our models quite prominent.

Boxcar roofs are usually galvanized steel. Into the 1960s, these roofs were commonly painted the car color. Over the years, the paint would wear away, revealing galvanized metal. This would start as small patches of silver/gray showing through. These patches would continue to grow until the entire roof – except for the raised caps between roof panels – was showing, sometimes with rust patches as well. The Chicago Great Western boxcar on page 84 is an example.

This effect is easy to re-create. Simply brush dull silver paint (I like Polly Scale Flat Aluminum) in patches on the roof. Vary the appearance among cars – no silver on some, light on others, and heavy on a few. Keep the silver off of the seam caps. The silver is actually rather bright for galvanized metal, but we'll fix that in a minute.

Once the silver is applied, finish weathering the roof. Don't overdo it – exposure to rain tends to wash away grime, so roofs aren't usually dirty. Instead, they are bleached by the sun, so the paint tends to fade and become dull.

7-19

The C&NW painted out the old Rock Island logo and lettering and restenciled new reporting marks, number, and herald on this boxcar.

Keith Kohlmann

7-20

A bit of paint and a few decals changed owners on this Athearn boxcar.

Tone down the silver and give it more of a dull galvanized look by brushing on gray chalk or giving the roof a light overspray of thinned gray or grimy black paint. You can see examples of roofs finished this way on page 62 and throughout this book.

You can treat modern roofs in much the same way. Although some modern roofs are painted, from the 1960s on, many galvanized roofs have been left unpainted. Some have an overspray of the car color around the edges, which can be captured by airbrushing a thinned mixture of the car color around the perimeter, **7-21**. Many models include silver roofs; tone these down with gray chalk or an overspray of grimy black, **7-21**.

As cars age, the galvanized coating sometimes wears off, and the roof begins rusting, **7-22**. Model this by painting patches of various rust colors on the roof, then blending them with chalk or an overspray of gray to grimy black, **7-23**. Again, vary this appearance among cars.

Final thoughts

To avoid falling into a rut when weathering cars, try different techniques. Varying appearances among cars makes them more interesting. And, most importantly, don't be afraid to try new techniques – but always try out new methods on a scrap shell or swap-meet car before weathering a prize model.

7-22

Rust is taking over on the roof of this Norfolk & Western boxcar.

Tank car weathering

Tank cars sometimes show distinctive stains left by their loads. One example is the molten sulfur car shown in chapter 6. Weathering it was a matter of blending a yellow-green mix to represent the loading spills of elemental sulfur. The effect is the result of a combination of airbrushing the stain around the manway and brushing it down the sides, along with streaking black back over the yellow-green.

Keep an eye on real cars for ideas. Phosphoric acid cars have white streaks; asphalt, tar, and oil cars will have shiny black spills that contrast with the flat grime of day-to-day weathering; other cars acquire a rusty cast.

Acrylic weathering colors

Both Polly Scale (PS) and Badger Modelflex (MF) offer a variety of acrylic paints designed specifically for weathering, including

- Rust (PS 414323, MF 16172)
- Roof Brown (PS 414329, MF 16176)
- Rail Brown (MF 16175)
- Railroad Tie Brown (PS 414329)
- Grimy Black (PS 110013, MF 1603)
- Oily Black (PS 414326)
- Earth (PS 110081, MF 16174)
- Mud (PS 110083)
- Grime (PS 110086)

7-21

Tone down the bright silver roofs of factory-painted models with an overspray of grimy black. You can also add a light spray of the car color around the edge of the roof.

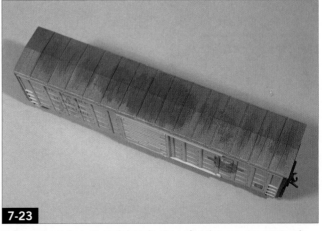

7-23

Paint rust patches on model roofs, then give them an overspray of grimy black.

CHAPTER EIGHT

Freight car loads

Adding a scale coal load to this N scale Micro-Trains hopper car, along with a bit of weathering, greatly improved its appearance.

Open cars – flatcars, gondolas, and hoppers – are fascinating to model because you can see what they're carrying. Many manufacturers offer commercial loads, but these can be improved, and a wide choice of materials and techniques for making your own loads can give your cars and your layout a unique touch.

8-1

Give the load a thick coat of black paint, then press scale coal in place over the paint.

8-2

Clean up the edges so that the load fits into the car.

Coal

Coal is so important to railroading both as a source of power and as a commodity that Accurail, Athearn, Chooch, Kadee, and others make coal loads for specific cars in HO, N, and other scales, and some manufacturers include loads with their cars. In many cases, these loads can be improved, and with a little work, you can even make your own loads.

Let's start by improving a commercial load. I grabbed several injection-molded styrene loads offered by Accurail for its own HO scale USRA hopper and for the Athearn two-bay car, but the fol-lowing technique will work with other manufacturers' loads in any scale.

Accurail's loads are designed to simply rest in the car. Steel ball bearings fit in pockets on the underside of the load, adding a bit of weight and enabling the loads to be removed by a magnet. The load's biggest problem is that the cast plastic looks more like the material it's made of than coal. This is a common problem with many bulk loads, whether plastic, plaster, or resin.

Let's begin by covering it with a thick coat of black paint. While the paint is still wet, pour scale coal over the load and press it down with your fingers, 8-1. Leave the excess in place and set the load aside overnight until the paint is dry.

Shake off the excess coal (be sure to save it for another load). Use a hobby knife to remove any stray paint and coal from the sides of the load, where it would interfere with the fit in the car, 8-2, and you're done.

Note that all coal isn't alike. Coal loads – especially in the steam era – ranged from fine lumps, about an inch in diameter, to "mine-run" coal several inches across, each with its own use, 8-3. Woodland Scenics, Faller, Noch, and others offer scale coal in various

8-3

The Accurail B&O car received fine coal, while the Athearn Illinois Central car is loaded with "mine-run" coal.

sizes, making it easy to capture these variations.

You can use a similar technique to make your own loads. Start with a piece of extruded foam (insulation board) or foam core, cutting it to fit into the car. I used this technique for the N scale Micro-Trains hopper on page 72, but you can make loads in any scale. Use a hobby knife to carve the top to the proper contour, **8-4**. Once the shape is correct, treat it the same as the commercial load, coating it with black paint followed by a coat of scale coal.

You can use the same techniques to model almost any bulk shipment including limestone, ballast, crushed rock, and sand.

Lumber loads

Lumber rode in boxcars, gondolas, and flatcars (standard and bulkhead) through the 1960s. Since that time, the center-beam flatcar has become the standard car for carrying lumber.

Today, most lumber is shipped in strapped bundles, and much of it is wrapped. Through the early diesel era,

many loads were made up of loose boards stacked and framed in place.

Commercial open and wrapped lumber loads are made by American Model Builders, Jaeger, and others. Some of these are scale lumber or laser-cut strips and sheets, while others are resin castings. Whether you use these or make your own loads, it's important to load your cars in a realistic manner.

Let's start by modeling an open lumber load for a flatcar. I used a Micro-Trains N scale 50-foot flatcar, but this technique works in any scale. You can go through a lot of wood in a hurry if you build loads with scale lumber. Minimize this problem by selecting larger stripwood or, as I did, by building hollow lumber stacks.

I made a two-tiered load of Midwest .0416"-square strips (no. 8016) for the smaller (top) lumber and .0416" x .0625" (no. 8017) strips for the bottom lumber. I cut the lower strips a scale 20 feet long; the top strips are a scale 16 feet long, but you can adjust this to fit your flatcar.

I piled up enough strips so that the load fits just inside the side stake holes on the flatcar – 15 boards in my case. I cut a layer of strips at a time with a NorthWest Short Line Chopper, **8-5**, which greatly speeds the process.

These loads usually weren't stacked in perfect alignment, and after being jostled by brake and slack action, boards often slid more out of line as they traveled. This irregular appearance gives the loads character and makes them interesting to model.

Build with the load upside-down, so you're actually building it top to bottom. A piece of tape holds the top layer of strips in place on your workbench, **8-6**. Cut shorter pieces and glue them on the ends of the stacks. White glue works well, but use it sparingly – apply it with a toothpick and wipe any glue that seeps from the joints.

Smaller cross strips (I used Midwest .0208" x .0312", no. 8001) separate each load into two or three tiers, **8-7**. Attach the finished loads with cyanoacrylate adhesive (CA) to the flatcar deck, centered lengthwise and between the stake pockets.

8-4

Foam is easy to carve into shaped bases for coal and other bulk loads.

8-5

A Chopper speeds the cutting process. You can cut several pieces of stripwood at once.

Place scale 4 x 4s (Midwest .0208"-square, no. 8000) in the stake pockets, using three or four per side per load (you may have to drill out the stake pockets to get them to fit), **8-7**. Glue them with CA. Trim them above the load, then connect these posts across the top of the load with .0208" x .0312" strips glued in place with white glue, **8-8**. Add lengthwise strips along the stakes, and the car is complete, **8-9**.

Center-beam bundled loads

Center-beam cars have been in service in large numbers since the 1970s for carrying lumber and finished lumber products, **8-10**. The cars make loading and unloading easy and provide a handy means of anchoring the loads.

Loads consist of strapped bundles of dimensional lumber, which may be wrapped or unwrapped. Several companies, including Walthers, make center-beam cars in HO and N scales. Walthers also makes simulated wrapped-lumber loads. The Walthers load has two injection-molded styrene

halves that fit on each side of the car and snap together in the middle. The overall effect is decent, but a bit of additional work will create a more-realistic car and load.

Brake gear is readily seen on these cars, so I started by adding brake piping and rodding as in chapter 3. I

also added new sill steps (chapter 4), consolidated stencils (chapter 6), and an AEI tag (chapter 4).

To improve the load itself, start by adding a thin wash of black paint (one part Polly Scale Steam Power Black, nine parts Polly S Airbrush Thinner) between the bundles, **8-11**. Load the

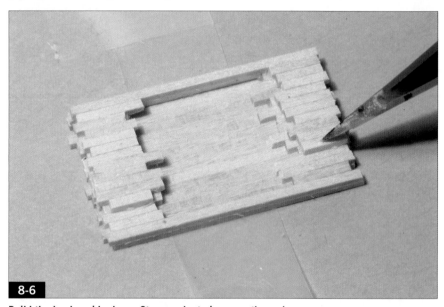

8-6
Build the load upside down. Stagger short pieces on the ends.

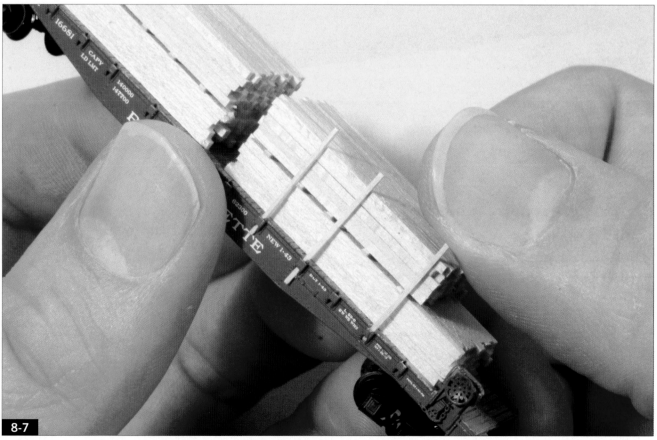

8-7
Small crosswise pieces separate the load into tiers. Press the side posts into the stake pockets on the car.

8-8

Glue small pieces from post to post across the top of the load, then add another strip lengthwise inside the side posts.

brush with the wash, then touch it to the grooves between the bundles. The dark grooves provide some separation between the bundles.

Paint the little knobs between the bundles, which represent spacers or separation strips. I used grimy black to represent weathered wood; you can use a lighter color for the look of new wood as well.

These loads must be firmly secured to the car, so the next step is to simulate the straps used on the real cars. Drill no. 61 holes in the "keyhole" slot top-strap anchors across the top beam of the car, **8-12**. These will hold the top of each strap in place. Set the load in place on the car.

8-9

The finished lumber load is quite distinctive.

8-10

Center-beam cars haul bundles of wrapped or exposed lumber. Note the cables that hold the loads in place.

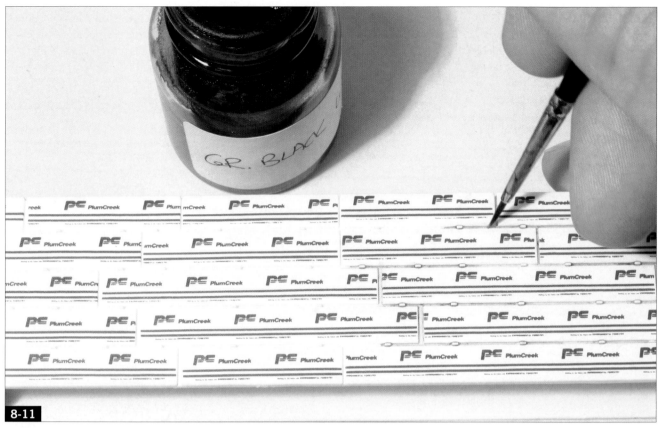

8-11

A grimy black wash in the gaps helps highlight the space between the bundles.

The best material I've found for the load cables is called EZ Line, an elastic thread made by Berkshire Junction. EZ Line is available in several colors, and it has many great model railroading applications. I used the fine black line for this car.

Cut several pieces of EZ Line so that each is about four-fifths of the distance between the sill strap anchor and the corresponding top anchor slot. With a toothpick, apply a bit of medium-thickness CA to the strap anchor on the side sill, then secure that end of the EZ Line in place, **8-13**, with tweezers.

Place a drop of CA in the top strap anchor hole. Use tweezers to pull the strap, placing the end into the CA in the hole, **8-14**. Hold it in place a few seconds until the glue sets. Repeat the process with the remaining straps. Brush some oily black paint into the side-sill strap anchors to kill any shine from the CA.

Small metal angles under the straps keep them from gouging the wood. I simulated these by painting a piece of

8-12

Drill out the anchor slots in the middle of the vertical beams (if you're building an empty car) or along the edge of the top beam (for a loaded car).

adhesive-backed Bare-Metal Foil grimy black, then cutting the foil into small (scale 6" or so) squares, **8-15**. Place a square under each cable where it passes over upper edge of the load. You could also use aluminum foil and glue the pieces in place with CA. Either way, the angles and cables make a big differ-

ence in the appearance of the finished car, **8-16**.

You can make individual wrapped bundles from kits from Jaeger, **8-17**, and others, or you can make your own on a computer and printer, perhaps starting with a digital image of a real load.

Center-beam exposed loads

Unwrapped lumber bundles also make distinctive loads. Just follow the method for making N scale flatcar loads shown earlier. Scale lumber looks great, but an inexpensive option for HO scale is bundles of craft wood, **8-18**. This material comes in many sizes and can be found in most craft stores.

Build the load with a hollow core as with the N scale car, but since the ends of the loads aren't visible, assembling the load around a solid core works well for center-beam cars. Start by cutting a

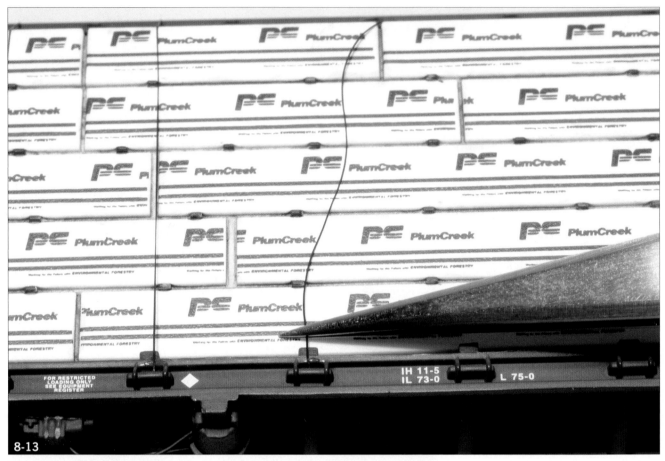

8-13
Use cyanoacrylate adhesive (CA) to glue one end of the EZ Line strap in the sill strap anchor.

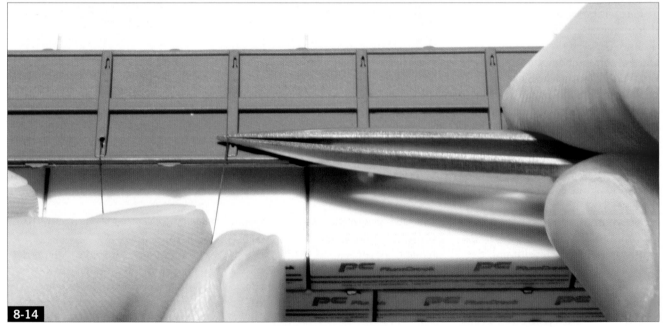

8-14
Place a drop of CA in the anchor slot, then set the end of the line into the slot with tweezers.

piece of wood as long as the bulkhead-to-bulkhead length of the car, and slightly shorter and narrower than the finished load. Be sure the load will fit inside the side sill. I used plywood, but dimensional lumber will work as well.

My craft wood strips measured about 1/16" square and 2½" long. This translates to an HO scale 6 x 6 – a healthy piece of lumber, but within reason for a model. Real dimensional lumber comes in many lengths of four-foot increments, with 8, 12, and 16 feet lengths common. Loads generally match the length of the car, so this 72-foot-long car can carry six 12-foot-long bundles, nine 8-foot-long bundles, or a combination of lengths adding up to 72 feet.

Cut several strips to the desired length. A Chopper makes quick work of it. Place a few drops of CA on the core and begin gluing strips onto it from the bottom up, **8-19**. Rust-color EZ line simulates the strapping by glu-

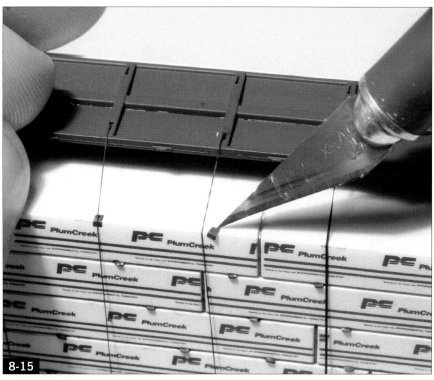

8-15

Small pieces of Bare-Metal Foil represent the metal angles that protect the load from the straps.

8-16

The straps give the car lacy detail that the stock factory model lacked.

Jaeger makes wrapped lumber loads in HO (shown) and N scale, consisting of wood blocks with printed paper wrappers.

ing two pieces of EZ line to the bottom strip. I made my bundles three and four strips tall. Add bits of stripwood at the top of each bundle to model the real pieces that separate the bundles.

Repeat the process with each column of stripwood, carrying the strips up and over the top of the core. If the height of the stacks is slightly off, you can glue a piece of thin sheet wood across the top of the core to match the height of the stacked strips.

Glue the load in place on the car, then add EZ Line straps over the load as with the bundled load, **8-20**.

EZ Line works great to detail an empty car, **8-21**. Drill no. 61 holes in the middle strap guides in the vertical posts, **8-12**. Run lengths of line from the sill strap guides through the middle of a post (three partitions to the side of the sill guide) to a guide on the other sill, **8-22**. The line nicely captures the lacy effect of the real cars, **8-23**.

Machinery loads

Flatcars haul lots of interesting equipment like tractors and bulldozers. Models of this heavy equipment are commonly available in hobby stores and catalogs, but to make them realistic as loads, they must be secured like the prototypes.

Machinery isn't just placed on the car, **8-24**. *Model Railroader* Senior Editor Jim Hediger modeled a heavy equipment load on an HO flatcar, **8-25**, which shows how wheels should be blocked and chained.

I gave similar treatment to a pair of Athearn John Deere tractors (one Model 50 and one Model 60), and placed them on a Proto 2000 flatcar

Packs of craft wood can be an inexpensive alternative to scale stripwood for making lumber loads.

8-19

Glue strips of wood to the stained wood core. EZ Line simulates the strapping around each bundle, with bits of smaller stripwood separating the bundles.

8-20

The finished loads look like solid bundles of lumber.

8-21

Run the EZ line through the middle strap anchor hole to a sill strap anchor on the other side.

with an American Model Builders wood deck (added in chapter 5), **8-26**. You can do the same with different loads depending upon your interests and the era you model.

Boxcar grain doors and loads

Well into the 1960s, 40-foot boxcars were the primary means of hauling grain by rail, **8-27**. Eventually, covered hoppers took over this traffic in large numbers, but boxcars continued hauling grain through the 1980s. Boxcars also hauled other bulk loads, such as flour and sugar.

Modeling a grain car adds interest to a grain elevator scene, and modeling an empty grain car with open doors provides an interesting look to a train.

To modify a boxcar for hauling grain, temporary wood or paper "grain doors" were nailed inside the door opening. Grain was then dumped into the car over the grain doors and the car's doors closed for shipping. At its destination, the car doors were opened, then the grain doors were ripped or knocked open, and the grain dropped

8-22

Empty center-beam cars reveal a lacy web of load-restraint cables.

8-23

The finished model captures the webbed look of the prototype car.

8-24

Equipment loads on flatcars are securely chained and secured to the deck.

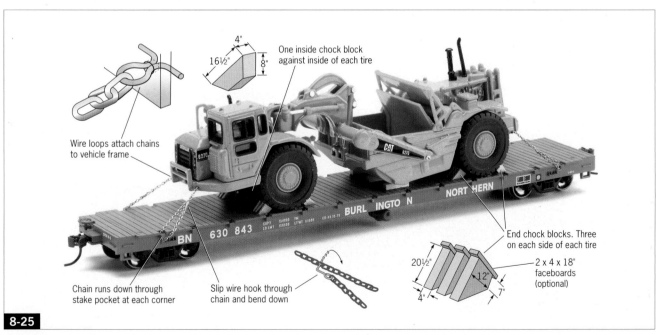

8-25

Jim Hediger fastened this Norscott model of a Caterpillar scraper to an HO Athearn flatcar following prototype practice. Eye bolts on the model provide connection points for the A-Line 40-links-per-inch chain.

8-26

A pair of HO scale Athearn tractors are firmly secured to a Proto 2000 flatcar.

into trackside receiving bins. Some large elevators used rotary dumpers.

Wood grain doors were the most common. They could be reused, so they often had a weathered appearance. Each wood door measured 20" to 36" tall, so multiple doors were nailed in place to obtain the proper height, which varied by the grain. Dense grains like corn would max out a car's weight

at a lower level (about 5"-6"), but light products like oats could be loaded to much higher levels.

Modeler's Choice offers wood grain doors in HO, but they're also easy to scratchbuild. To make wood grain doors, cut several lengths of scale 2 x 6 stripwood into pieces about two feet longer than the width of the door opening. Weather the stripwood with a thin wash

of black, grimy black, or roof brown paint. Since each door was made of multiple pieces (three or four) of wood, each set of three boards should be similarly weathered.

Glue the stripwood pieces edge to edge with CA or white glue, **8-28**. You can use a backing sheet of thin (.005" or .010") styrene to make gluing easier and the door sturdier, but don't put

8-27

Boxcars like this Chicago Great Western 40-footer with a wood grain door could be seen hauling grain into the 1980s. Richard Cecil

8-28

Temporary grain doors are unique to grain-hauling boxcars. Glue the 2 x 6 strips edge to edge. The styrene backing is optional.

8-29

For modeling a loaded car, you only need to install the walls above the height of the load.

8-30

Glue the finished grain door in place in the door opening. This is an HO scale InterMountain car.

backing on the door if it will be seen from behind.

Installing the door is simply a matter of gluing it inside the door opening, **8-30**. CA attaches the installation permanently, or white glue allows you to remove it. Depending upon the model you choose, you may have to modify the car's door to clear the grain door.

Paper grain doors with load
Modeling a car complete with a grain load will give you a distinctive, unusual car. I started with an HO scale Kadee PS-1 boxcar, and since the interior

of the car would be partially visible, I added a laser-cut boxcar interior kit from Red Caboose (no. 800008).

Stain this as described for the flatcar deck in chapter 5. You won't need the interior kit's floor, but the inside walls will be visible above the halfway point. Press to secure the peel-and-stick backing to the interior walls, making sure they're in proper alignment, **8-29**.

The boxcar door may require modification, depending on the make of your car. The lower door guide on each Kadee door needs to be removed, as it won't clear the grain door. The door

can be glued in position later.

Although never as popular as wood, paper doors could be seen from the late 1950s through the 1980s. These single-use doors were made of heavy paper or card, reinforced by steel strapping. Jaeger makes two styles of paper grain doors. I used set no. 2000, based on prototype doors made by Signode, **8-31**. Paper doors required a wood plank at the base, so start by gluing a scale 2 x 6 across the bottom of the door opening. Make sure that this piece will clear (but rest upon) the floor when the body is in place.

8-31

Cut the Jaeger doors to the proper height – seven feet on this car.

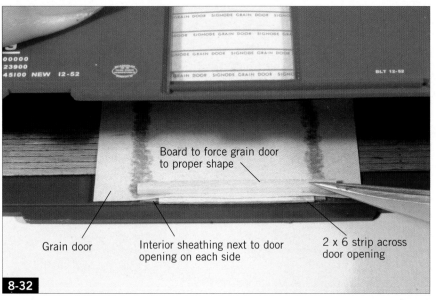

8-32

Board to force grain door to proper shape

Grain door

Interior sheathing next to door opening on each side

2 x 6 strip across door opening

Glue the paper door in place over the 2 x 6 across the door opening, then add a board across the rear of the grain door.

8-33

The grain door is in place across the door opening.

Next, cut the paper door to the desired height (usually 5-7 feet) and about two scale feet wider than the opening (my door was cut wider than it should have been). I would recommend gluing the door in place with Micro Kristal Klear, not the CA I used. A strip of wood across the rear of the door, **8-32**, will force it to the proper shape up and over the board at the bottom, **8-33**.

Shape the grain load from a piece of foam core in the same fashion as the coal load described earlier. Cut the foam a few scale feet shorter than the car and so it fits snugly from side to side without causing the sides to bow outward. Contour the top with a hobby knife, giving it a gently undulating appearance, **8-34**.

Use a brush to paint the foam with Polly Scale Depot Buff paint, a dull yellow. Be sure to work the paint into all the undulations in the foam. When it dries, it will have a color and texture that nicely simulates a load of wheat or corn.

Fit the load into place, making sure to keep it below the top of the grain doors. Glue it in place with CA, adding small lengths of plastic or wood strip to reinforce the joint, **8-35**. The resulting car is shown in **8-36**.

Empty grain cars also have a distinct look, and they could often be found riding the rails with their doors open and the remains of their paper doors visible.

Since the car interior will show, install and weather a car interior (or make your own from scribed wood or styrene) for the walls and floor.

Paper doors were hacked opened on one side with a hatchet, so you can slash your model grain door with a hobby knife to simulate the same look. These doors had steel strapping across the back. If your paper door will be visible from behind, simulate this by gluing lengths of EZ Line to the back, **8-37**. (It would be visible if both boxcar doors are open, if the grain door is folded in, or it is torn and placed on the floor.)

Glue the two pieces of the grain door in place on either side of the door opening. Push back and wrinkle the wide side to simulate a door that's been pushed back in after unloading. You can also tear part of the door away and glue it to the floor.

8-34

Paint the carved foam core load with Polly Scale Depot Buff.

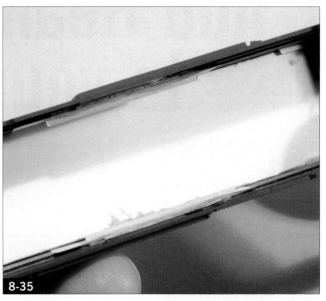

8-35

Glue the foam core load in place, using a couple of wood or styrene reinforcing strips.

Simulate stray grain by brushing some light yellow chalk on the car floor. Your car is now ready to enhance an elevator scene or equally ready to roll in a freight back to a rural elevator for reloading, **8-38**.

It's all in your imagination

The ideas in this chapter (and in the entire book for that matter) barely scratch the surface of possibilities for detailing, weathering, and improving freight cars. What you see here are suggestions to stimulate your imagination. As ever, prototype equipment and practices make the best examples.

8-36

The finished car is ready to enhance an elevator scene.

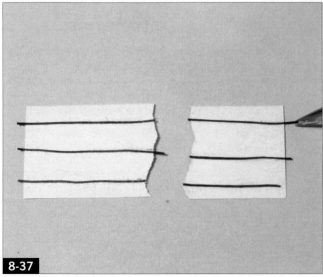

8-37

Lengths of EZ line glued across the back simulate the steel strapping of prototype paper grain doors.

8-38

The finished car looks great at an elevator or riding in a train back to harvest country.

Add Realistic Details to your Layout!

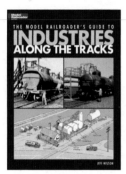

The Model Railroader's Guide to Industries Along the Tracks

Provides model railroaders with an overview of North American mining, refining, and agricultural operations served by the railroads, and the specific techniques used to model them on a realistic layout of any scale. Numerous photos and illustrations show key structures, the sequence of operations, and details. By Jeff Wilson. 8-¼ x 10-¾; 88 pgs.; 50 color and 150 black & white photos; 20 illus.; softcover.

12256 • $19.95

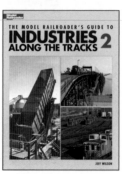

The Model Railroader's Guide to Industries Along the Tracks 2

Add realism to your layout! Jeff Wilson provides insights, photos, and guidelines for modeling several rail-served industries. Includes overviews of creameries and milk traffic, the paper industry, breweries, iron ore mining and transloading, freight houses and less-than-carload traffic, and coal customers. 8-¼ x 10-¾; 88 pgs.; 62 color and 102 b&w photos; 4 illus.; softcover.

12409 • $19.95

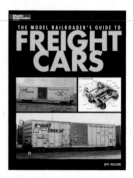

The Model Railroader's Guide to Freight Cars

Freight cars are the backbone of any railroad – in the real world or on your operating layout. Get a brief history of each type of North American freight car, then learn how car designs have changed from WWI to the present. Includes techniques for modeling realistic rolling stock in any scale. By Jeff Wilson. 8-½ x 10-¾; 96 pgs.; 75 color and 110 black & white photos; 15 illus.; softcover.

12450 • $19.95

Every issue includes intriguing articles that take you on a tour of the world's finest layouts and introduce you to the hobby's experts. You'll also discover a wealth of prototype data, detailed how-to instructions, product reviews, tips, techniques, and so much more! 12 issues per year

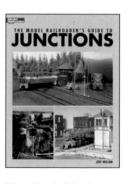

The Model Railroader's Guide to Junctions

Add interest to your layout! Photos of different types of prototype junctions with details about how they work give you the inside scoop on junctions. Learn to model junctions and the details around them with expert instruction from Jeff Wilson. 8-¼ x 10-¾; 88 pgs.; 30 color and 150 b&w photos; 20 illus.; softcover.

12408 • $18.95

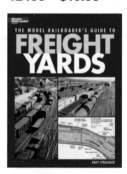

The Model Railroader's Guide to Freight Yards

HO and N scale illustrations plus prototype and layout photos introduce modelers to designing, constructing, and operating a realistic freight yard. Covers how rail yards receive and classify trains; defines yard designs and structures; and offers techniques for modeling yards. By Andy Sperandeo. 8-½ x 10-¾; 80 pgs.; 50 color and 100 black & white photos; 40 illus.; softcover.

12248 • $18.95